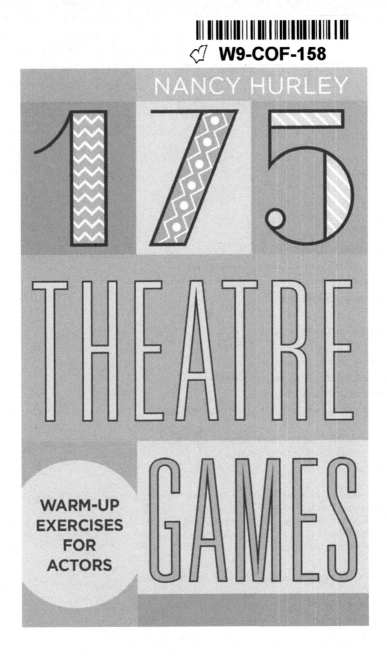

NANCY HURLEY

175

THEATRE

GAMES

WARM-UP
EXERCISES
FOR
ACTORS

MERIWETHER PUBLISHING
A division of Pioneer Drama Service, Inc.
Denver, Colorado

Meriwether Publishing
A division of Pioneer Drama Service, Inc.
PO Box 4267
Englewood, CO 80155

www.pioneerdrama.com

Editor: Arthur L. Zapel
Assistant editor: Amy Hammelev
Cover design: Devin Watson
Interior photos and illustrations: Nancy Hurley

Library of Congress Cataloging-in-Publication Data

Hurley, Nancy, 1946-
    175 theatre games : warm-up exercises for actors / by Nancy Hurley. -- 1st ed.
        p. cm.
Includes bibliographical references.
    ISBN 978-1-56608-164-1 (alk. paper)
1. Drama in education. 2. Acting--Study and teaching. I. Title. II. Title: One hundred and seventy-five theatre games.
PN3171.H87   2009
792.02'807--dc22

                                        2009021932

12   13   14   23   24   25

Table of Contents

Acknowledgements

My dear husband, Patrick, for his enthusiastic support, wise advice, continuous encouragement, and hours of proofreading.

My former students who proved to me the importance of warm-up games and who were always willing to try a new game.

Jacquelyn Karney and her students for playing many of the games and being willing to be photographed.

Marilyn Pugh for her enthusiastic response to my requests and theatrical ventures.

The clever game players (whoever and wherever they are) who created and shared the games in this book.

Foreword

In 1991, when I was Principal of Diegueño Middle School in Encinitas, California, I hired Nancy Hurley as our drama teacher. I *love* middle school, and I realized that Nancy did too. She came enthusiastically prepared with ideas, games, exercises, and activities to capture the imaginations of middle school students.

It was magic to see her on the stage, working with future actors and actresses. Some students were natural performers and loved being in theatre class from the moment they entered the classroom. Others, who did not receive their first or second elective choice, resisted the idea of doing anything related to theatre.

Nancy Hurley wove her magic with all her students, theatre lovers or not. She began each semester and many subsequent classes with ice breakers and games in order to get students participating, talking with each other, and feeling comfortable in front of others. Most students knew little about pantomime so mime activities became favorites. Also, her clowning unit was popular, especially since the students warmed up with funny games, clowned around in goofy skits, put on makeup, and created colorful costumes for their performances.

I firmly believe that there is a bit of a junior high student in all of us so this book will be useful to anyone who reads it. As readers peruse the table of contents and review the delightful games, they will find that most of them can be adapted to any age group: elementary, middle school, high school, or adult "kids."

In this book, readers will be exposed to and rewarded with some excellent interactive strategies. No matter how old they are, as they take part in the warm-up games, students will have the opportunity to use their creativity and imagination to laugh and to learn something about themselves and about the others in their group or class. I hope many become part of the fun, the laughter, the imagination, and the creativity that Nancy Hurley intended.

Marilyn Pugh
Retired Principal
Diegueño Middle School
Encinitas, CA

Introduction

When asked by her counselor to name her favorite class, one of my Introduction to Theatre students enthusiastically replied, "Theatre."

"Why is it your favorite?" the counselor asked.

"Because we get to play games!" she exclaimed.

When students arrive for a theatre class they are ready for and appreciate a game or exercise that will loosen them up and activate their right brain — the artistic side. A good warm-up gives class members the opportunity to tune in to their creative natures and readies them for the adventures ahead.

The games and exercises in this book are designed to be used as warm-ups at the beginning of a theatre class period. They are organized into sections that focus on specific skills, such as concentration or pantomime.

The games have been played successfully with middle school students and could be adapted for use with younger children, older teens, and adults in other settings.

Some benefits of incorporating warm-ups at the beginning of a class would be to:

• Encourage creativity and the use of imagination
• Foster cooperation and teamwork
• Instill confidence and a strong self-image
• Provide unique interaction with peers
• Increase focus and concentration
• Improve listening skills
• Encourage acceptance of each student's uniqueness
• Allow fun and humor to permeate the classroom

Over the past nine years of teaching middle school I've adapted games from theatre games books, theatre and acting workshops, improvisation exercises found on websites, recreational games books, children's playground games, and from old standard camp activities. As a result of my research I've created this book of warm-up games. They can be played in a regular classroom, a gym, on a stage, or in any fairly large area.

My criteria have been that: they actively involve most, if not all, of the students in a class; the directions are not complicated and can be easily implemented; accomplish my goals; my students enjoy them.

Throughout the book I have used the pronoun "he" when referring to a singular student so that "he/she" doesn't appear repeatedly.

The games are arranged in alphabetical order in each section. The introduction to each section is to provide a bit of background or history on the subject and to elucidate the purpose behind playing the games. There are hundreds, perhaps thousands, of theatre games used by theatre teachers for a variety of purposes and most of the games can be woven into a theatre curriculum as learning exercises.

If any of the games included in this book seem familiar to you it's because games have a way of being passed from one person to another. They may not be explained or played the way you remember them because I've taken the liberty of adapting and revising them to fit my own teaching situation. At the end of the book is a bibliography, including books and web sites. It's often difficult to give credit where it is due because many of the games have been passed on without mention being made of the creator. Thanks to all those who have shared games by publishing them or teaching them to me. It is with pleasure that I pass them on to be used in new ways with new players.

Chapter One
Clowning

"Be a clown, be a clown, all the world loves a clown."
— Cole Porter

Clowning is an ancient theatrical form. The first recorded clown performance was around 3000 BC in ancient Egypt and court jesters are known to have performed in China as early as 1818 BC.
Today's clowns are much like the medieval court jesters who were often versatile physical performers with many tricks up their sleeves. They were trained in a variety of skills in order to keep the fickle royalty entertained: contortion, magic, juggling, acrobatics, storytelling, puppetry, tightrope walking, exhibiting trained animals, ballad singing, and clever dialogue. Also called "the fool," the court jester wore a bright, multi-colored costume which may have been the inspiration for the clown costumes of today.

Recognized for their contribution to the art of clowning, many clowns worldwide have been inducted into the Clown Hall of Fame. Several familiar names are: Joseph Grimaldi, the father of modern clowning; Dan Rice, the model for Uncle Sam; Lou Jacobs, creator of the midget car; Emmett Kelly, the most well-known of the tramp clowns; Bozo the Clown; Red Skelton; Bob Keeshan, the first to play Clarabell on the '50s TV show, *The Howdy Doody Show.*

Because clowning involves so many varied theatrical skills, it makes perfect sense to provide theatre students with the chance to create either an informal clown skit or a polished clowning performance, which could include magic, juggling, storytelling, singing, and clever repartee.

To dovetail an experience in practicing pantomime, theatre students have the opportunity to refine their use of exaggerated movement and facial expression in a unit on clowning.

Warm-ups in this section are mostly adapted from relay races and games that lend themselves to exaggeration. They are predominantly used for a physical warm-up that encourages speed, dexterity, and quick thinking — the skills and qualities a versatile actor needs to create a clown character. They also encourage team effort with lots of cheering and laughter.

1. Balloon Sandwich

Balloons are usually associated with clown antics. Only clowns would make a balloon sandwich!

Materials: A package of large, round balloons

For this race, the group is divided into pairs who line up back to back at the starting line.

A balloon is placed between the partners' backs so that they must squeeze it, keeping it off the ground, not using their hands. At the sound of a whistle, or any other cue, the pairs make their way toward a finish line. If the balloon pops or drops, the players must return to the starting line where they are given a replacement or their balloon will be repositioned. The first balloon sandwich to cross the finish line wins.

2. Bobbity Balloon Relay

A balloon can be hard to keep track of, therefore providing lots of giggles.

Materials: A package of balloons

The group is divided into teams of ten or twelve. Half of each team is at opposite ends of the room, at least twenty feet apart. The first player of each team is presented with a balloon and races to his team at the other end of the room while keeping the balloon in the air without holding it — he taps or lightly bounces the balloon in the air. When a player reaches the other side, the balloon is passed off to the first player in line, who then races back to the other line, passes it off to the next person, and so on. If a player grasps the balloon with both hands at any time or the balloon touches the ground, he is sent back to the front of his line and must repeat his turn to get to the other side while keeping the balloon in the air. To be declared the winners *all* members of the team must have successfully raced with the balloon in the air the whole time.

3. Clown Class Relay

A clown costume is usually a source of laughter, let alone watching someone try to get into one fast!

Materials: Two clown outfits consisting of: a giant shirt, giant pants, a hat, a large jacket, and a large pair of men's shoes or clown shoes

Preparation: The teacher places two clown outfits at the other end of the room on a clearly marked line. Players are barefoot or wearing socks.

The group is divided into two teams positioned at a starting line, opposite the clown clothes at the other end of the room. At the sound of a goofy noise-maker, the first person from each team runs, puts on the clown outfit over his clothes, runs back to his line, takes off the clown outfit as quickly as possible, tags the next player who then puts on the outfit, runs to the line on which the clown clothes were first set at the other end of the room, runs back to the line, and so on.

When the last player on a team is the first to take off the clown outfit, his team is declared the winner.

4. Draw a Face Race

Laughter is inevitable when students must quickly draw their own face.

Materials: Crayons and two pads of drawing paper

Preparation: The crayons and pads of drawing paper are placed at one end of the room.

The players are split into two teams who stand in a single file behind the starting line, on the opposite side of the room from the paper and crayons. When a cue is given, the relay begins. The first player from each team runs to the paper and crayons, draws his face on a pad, signs his name, puts the pad and pencil back down, and runs back to tag the next runner. The team that finishes their face drawings first wins. The fun comes when everyone tries to identify the faces drawn by the contestants.

5. The Exaggeration Game

This is a pantomime game turned into a clowning warm-up.

Preparation: The teacher needs to prepare a list of simple actions. *Theatre Games for Young Performers* by Maria C. Novelly from Meriwether Publishing is a great source for ideas.

Players get into a big circle *or* they can find their own spot somewhere in the classroom, staying three to five feet away from any other player. When a simple action or movement is called out, the students perform it. They should be instructed to exaggerate it, which is what clowns do to create humor. For example, if the players are instructed to tiptoe, they wouldn't do it as they do in real life, but would pretend they're a clown on tiptoe, holding their finger to their lips, looking around to see if anyone is watching, lifting their knees high, and letting their foot come down toe to heel, à la *The Three Stooges*.

Actions to Exaggerate
Watching a scary movie
Walking a dog
Pulling a piece of bubble gum out of your hair
Receiving a wonderful surprise gift
Having a toothache
Performing as a ballerina
Lifting a very heavy barbell

6. Michelin Man

The students will love to transform each other into the Michelin Man!

Materials: Two huge white shirts and several packages of balloons

The players are divided into two teams positioned at opposite sides of the room. Each team chooses one player to be the Michelin Man, who puts on a huge white shirt. The rest of the team receives a bag of new balloons. At the command "go," they blow them up all the way — partially inflated balloons are not acceptable — and fill the Michelin Man's shirt with them. The teacher decides on a time limit, and when the time is up, the team with the most balloons in their Michelin Man's shirt wins.

7. Paper Training Relay

This relay looks easy until students try it. Let the laughter begin!

Materials: A pile of newspapers

The group is divided into two teams. Half of each team is at one end of the room, and half are at the other. The first player on each team is handed two sheets of newspaper. When the cue is given to begin, the first player on each team places a sheet of newspaper on the floor and steps on it, then puts down the second sheet and steps on that. He must then reach back, pick up the first piece of paper and put it down before taking another step. No one is allowed to take a step that isn't on newspaper! This process is repeated all the way to an awaiting teammate at the other end of the room who uses the newspaper in the same way to walk to his teammate at the other end, and so on. When newspapers become too torn and shredded to walk on, they can be replaced with new ones. The first team to have their last player walk to their first player wins.

8. Pass the Hula Hoop

This game encourages agility and cooperation in a fun and silly way.

Materials: Several hula hoops

Players get into a big circle and hold hands. Two people let go and place their hands through a hula hoop before rejoining their hands. The object of the game is to pass the hula hoop around the circle and back to where it started without the group letting go of each others' hands. Everyone will enjoy watching as the hula hoop is maneuvered around the circle by each player.

Variation 1: Play using two hoops and pass them in opposite directions.

Variation 2: Play an upbeat song for fifteen seconds at a time. When the music stops, the player who has the hula hoop around his body is out. Play until one player is left. This variation is fun because as the players are eliminated they gather around to cheer for those who are left.

Variation 3: Play with two groups competing against each other.

9. Rumor

Get ready for a clown chuckle at the end of this game! Remember, it's not safe to believe any rumor without tracing it back to the source.

Materials: Index cards, a basket

Preparation: The teacher writes proverbs, lines from a movie or song, or original sentences on index cards and places them in the basket.

The class is divided into two equal teams who stand single file. The player at the head of each line picks a message out of the basket. At a signal from the teacher, the first player whispers the message to the next player. The message is then whispered player to player until the last person in line receives it.

When each team is finished, the last player says aloud to the whole group the message he received. Then the player at the head of the line reads out loud the original message. The team that gets the message correct, or the closest to being correct, wins. The last player in each line then moves to the front and draws a new message from the basket, and the "rumors" continue. The players may want to play several times.

10. Sock Mania

What a fun warm-up for a unit on clowning or any situation in which lively participation is desired!

Materials: A large pile of at least thirty men's tube socks, a blindfold, and a stopwatch

Preparation: A player is chosen or volunteers to be the timer.

The class is split into two teams who sit on the floor. One player from each team participates at a time, while their teammates cheer them on. The representatives have their shoes off and the pile of socks is between them. The two players can pick one sock and have it ready to pull onto their foot before being blindfolded. When the person designated as the timer gives the signal, the players have one minute to see who can put the most socks on one foot.

After one minute, the timer says "stop," and each player counts how many socks he has on his foot. The timer, another student, or the teacher could act as tabulator. The socks are removed and put back in the pile, and the next representative from each team then puts on the socks. This warm-up is played until each team member has had a turn at the sock pile. The winner is the team who has put on the most socks.

Chapter Two
Cooperation and Teamwork

"Great discoveries and improvements invariably involve the
cooperation of many minds."
— Alexander Graham Bell

Putting on a play, rehearsing, or performing a scene requires a team effort. In theatre, teamwork is experienced when actors are successful in handling the acting and production tasks associated with a play performance.

The stages of play production — similar to a team sporting event — involve many people, many jobs, and a shared sense of excitement along with a sense of responsibility. Teamwork, no matter what the setting, engages individuals in a cooperative effort in order to achieve a common objective.

A theatre director acts as organizer, orchestrator, and motivator for the production crew — the members of the team who look after lights, sets, props, and sound to create the environment for a performance — and the cast.

The actors are inspired by the director and are coached to bring their characters to life on stage. With a cooperative spirit, everyone contributes something essential to ensure that audience members are entertained and that their minds and imaginations are stretched.

Most games encourage cooperation among players, but the warm-ups in this section are played specifically to foster both teamwork and cooperation.

11. Be a Household Appliance

This exercise is wonderful for teamwork, but it also works well during a unit on pantomime.

Materials: Index cards cut in half, a basket

Preparation: The teacher writes a name of an appliance on half an index card and puts the cards in the basket. There should be ten to fifteen appliance cards.

The players are arranged in groups of four to six. Each group draws a card from the basket. Their objective is to pantomime the appliance for their classmates. Each person within the group becomes a part of their appliance. If necessary, one player may operate the appliance, and if they choose, a sound effect may be used to enhance the performance. When rehearsals for the appliance have been accomplished, each group takes turns performing for the rest of the players, who then guess the appliance that has been portrayed.

Example
Six players could pantomime being a washing machine. To form the washer, one of them stands facing upstage with arms outstretched. Another player stands in the same position about three feet away, facing the first player. Two other players connect their hands to the first two players and face stage left and right — they look like a big square washer. The fifth player, the agitator, stands in the center of the washer. When the sixth actor pantomimes lifting the lid, dumping in clothes, pouring in detergent, turning the dial, and closing the lid, the fifth player lifts his elbows to a ninety degree angle in front of him, his palms touching, and turns his torso from left to right, making the sound, "Chooka chooka chooka."

Appliances
Toaster
Blender
Popcorn popper
Vacuum cleaner
Electric mixer

12. Circle Crescendo

In this warm-up, students work closely together to accomplish a common goal.

The players stand in a circle. Going around the circle, one person at a time, they count from one to the total number of students. The first person whispers "one" as quietly as possible, the next person says "two" a little louder, the next speaks a bit louder still, and so on until the last person in the group is reached, who is the loudest.

Each student must be careful not to make such a big jump in volume that the group reaches the extreme of loudness before the highest number is spoken. Conversely, care must also be taken not to make each increase so tiny that the last numbers to be said require large jumps in volume.

Variations: The group can use different extremes like loudest to softest, Mona Lisa smile to falling on the floor laughing, or slightly concerned to terrified.

13. Circle Mirror

This is the first of many "mirror" warm-ups.

The students stand in a circle, allowing room for free arm movement. As the mirror, the teacher stands anywhere in the circle and initiates slow, simple movements with his hands, arms, shoulders, head, legs, and combinations thereof for about thirty seconds, which the students imitate. The teacher then says "freeze," and the players stop moving. A student is then selected to become the mirror. The students imitate the motions of the new mirror. Play continues as long as students remain interested and movements are original.

14. Cooperative Ball Toss

Not only does this game foster cooperation, but it also encourages concentration and a good memory.

Materials: Several small soft balls and a container to hold them

The teacher and students stand in a large circle. The container of balls is placed in front of the teacher who makes eye contact with a student and throws a ball to him. That player then makes eye contact with someone else and throws the ball to him. Each person in the circle throws to a different person so that everyone in the circle has received and thrown the ball. A pattern is established.

After everyone has received and thrown one ball, the game is started again with the same ball. Everyone throws the ball to the same person that he threw it to in round one. It's important that everyone remember to whom they threw the ball and from whom they received it. In round two, after the ball has been thrown to several players, more balls are introduced. The pattern of throws is always the same, so ideally there is little if any confusion. Players always receive a ball from a certain person and throw it to a certain person.

The game can be played as long as desired. Perhaps balls could be subtracted from the circle until there are none left to throw, and that is the end of the game.

This game is magical if it's done quietly. The focus is on being alert to receiving the ball and keeping the throwing pattern rhythmically continuous.

15. Digits

This is a great game to cultivate timing, perception, and sharing. It is better not to impose regulations on the game so that students have the opportunity to learn to go with the flow.

The game can be played in a circle or with students sitting in rows of desks or chairs. It works best if everyone closes their eyes. The teacher begins the game by saying "one." Then someone — anyone — says "two," and so on. No one knows who will speak the next number. They *sense* when it is their turn to say a number.

If two people speak out at the same time, the game begins again. The goal is to count to twenty; however, since this is difficult, there will be great rejoicing when the group manages to count to ten!

16. Hot Spot

Being in the hot spot may provide students with the feeling of being a member of an encouraging group who enjoys supporting each other.

Materials: A list of well-known songs laminated or placed in a plastic cover

Preparation: A list of simple songs is compiled by the teacher, perhaps with the help of the students ahead of time.

Players stand in a circle. One player steps into the circle and starts singing a known song. The list of well-known songs is available to players to refer to in case they can't think of one. As soon as the singer shows any signs of stopping because he doesn't remember any more lines or gets tired, another player steps in and takes over, singing a different song. The idea is to keep singing, and the players get the experience of being supported by group members. The game can be played until everyone has had an opportunity to sing.

17. Knots

This game is like solving a puzzle while exercising cooperation and teamwork.

The students are divided into two *even* numbered groups spread throughout the room — six per group is ideal. Groups stand in a circle, facing inward. Players reach across the circle with their right hand and take hold of another player's right hand. They must *not* take hold of the hand of someone who is standing immediately to their right or left. After everyone is holding someone's right hand, they grab the left hand of someone different, but *not* someone who is standing immediately to their left or right. Then the signal is given to untangle their arms without letting go, although they may have to loosen their grip a little to allow for twisting and turning. After all the groups have successfully untangled themselves, they might enjoy a contest to see which group can finish untangling first.

18. Living Clay

Working together can produce an unusual and creative result.

Divide the class into groups of five or six. One person becomes the sculptor, and the others become the clay. The sculptor works with the bodies, intertwining limbs of the others in his group to form a sculpture, and then gives it a title such as

The Sunken Ship, Robot Housekeeper, or Table and Chairs. For a finale, some students, or a pair of students, could be chosen to make the world's largest living sculpture using the whole group as clay.

19. Transformations

Working together on a creative project engenders a cooperative spirit.

The class is divided into two teams. The goal of the game is for players to transform themselves into representations of whatever the teacher describes. The name of an object is called out and team members arrange themselves into that shape. For example, if the teacher says helicopter, players must decide how they will link together to form propellers, a cockpit, and landing gear.

Transformations continue until a time limit is reached or until the groups have accomplished two or three transformations.

Transformations

Suspension bridge
Ship
Cathedral
Tree
Truck
Bus
Skyscraper

20. Walk with Me

In theatre class there is usually lots of room for creative license, but in this warm-up, students experience the satisfaction of allowing another person to fulfill his creative vision.

Players stand in a circle with one in the middle. The player in the middle begins to walk in a distinct way. As the player walks, he invites another player to join him in the circle and mimic his walk by saying,

"Come walk with me." Once the two players have walked completely around the circle, one following the other, the person who initiated the walk rejoins the circle. The person who mimicked the walk begins a completely different walk and invites someone else to join him. If time permits, each player may have the opportunity to teach another player a distinct walk.

21. Zoom

The goal of this warm-up is to rapidly and rhythmically build and sustain group involvement.

The players stand in a circle and someone starts by saying "zoom" to the player on his right. Players focus on listening for "zoom" on their left and will immediately say "zoom" to the person on their right.

Variation 1: Pass the zoom the other direction.

Variation 2: Pass the zoom both to the right and left of the circle at the same time.

Variation 3: Pass a different word, students' choice.

Chapter Three
Focus and Concentration

"There can only be one state of mind as you approach any profound test; total concentration, a spirit of togetherness, and strength."

— Pat Riley

Focus and concentration are two important qualities that will help ensure that a student actor will be successful on the stage. According to Fran Averett Tanner in her book *Basic Drama Projects*, concentration is defined as "constant thought or attention to what one is doing; attentiveness." This is an excellent, perhaps rather idealistic definition because distractions are commonplace. For example, in an hour long class period a girl in the front row may sneeze, the phone often rings, a student could enter the door with a message from the administrative office, and a boy who looks very pale might ask for a pass to the nurse's office. Somehow, even though there are myriad interruptions, the lesson somehow gets taught. The real world is a sea of distractions, but as human beings we have learned how to reasonably exercise the art of concentration and get the job done.

An actor creates an imaginary world and must be detached from various distractions in his environment. The first commandment for an acting student is: Stay in character no matter what. However, "no matter what" can include many interesting challenges for a fledging thespian. A young inexperienced theatre student is often more concerned about how he's doing and how his peers are reacting to him than what his character is saying or doing. He may allow himself to be distracted by details unrelated to his purpose as an actor, or perhaps he hasn't learned to focus on the task at hand. Focus is important for an actor because when he concentrates on an object or person, the audience will pay attention. If not, the audience will lose interest because the action on-stage is not believable.

Constantin Stanislavski utilized a technique called *objects of attention*, which means that the actor, at every moment of a performance, knows where and what he should be concentrating on. Stanislavski worked with a technique called *circle of attention*, where an actor was asked to imagine himself on a pitch-black stage and suddenly a spotlight was turned on, creating a pool of light. Once he entered the pool of light he was isolated, nothing existed outside of it except empty blackness. The point that Stanislavski was making with this visualization was that when an actor is performing he must create his own circle of attention, which only includes the space in which he is performing. Everything outside ceases to exist. Stanislavski's approach to learning concentration is no doubt valuable but may be somewhat extreme.

In order to practice the concept of *aesthetic distance*, the awareness of, but detachment from the real world, an actor concentrates on his performance. He stays in character because he has learned to be aware of his exterior circumstance, mainly the audience, but not be affected by them.

The ability to focus and concentrate can be cultivated. The following games allow students to sharpen their ability to stick with the task at hand in a lighthearted way. It is possible through practice to learn to stay in character *no matter what.*

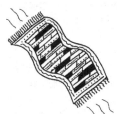

22. Ali Baba

It would be difficult to find a better game to exercise concentration skills!

Players stand or sit in a circle. A rhythm is established by repeating "Ali Baba and the forty thieves," all together until everyone is in unison. Then the teacher starts the game by saying in rhythm, "Ali Baba and the forty thieves," while making movements to the rhythm, such as snapping his fingers, clapping, or patting his head. The person to the teacher's right imitates the motion while saying, "Ali Baba and the forty thieves," and so on.

As soon as the first motion is moving around the circle, the teacher says "Ali Baba and the forty thieves," for the second time adding a new hand motion. The player on the teacher's right must keep an eye on the teacher because each time "Ali Baba and the forty thieves," is repeated, a new motion is started, and the player must duplicate it, and pass it around the circle.

The warm-up is finished when the teacher has received all the motions he sent around the circle. The more motions sent, the more potential distractions will have been created and the longer the game will take. It is easy to get lost if a player gets caught up in the many actions being sent around the circle. The key to lack of confusion is to watch the previous player and take over that gesture.

23. A What?

This warm-up has the potential of grabbing the attention of the entire group. Each player will enjoy the anticipation of engaging in the bit of dialogue with a partner.

Materials: A pen, a watch, a book, and other one-syllable word objects

The goal of the game is to pass an object(s) around the circle without breaking the rhythm of the script. The players stand or sit in a circle. One person, the Giver, offers an object to the person on the right, the Receiver, after the following bit of dialogue is completed:

GIVER: This is a pen.
RECEIVER: A what?
GIVER: A pen.
RECEIVER: A what?
GIVER: A pen.
RECEIVER: Oh, a pen. *(Takes the pen.)*

The Receiver now has the pen. The script is repeated by the Receiver, who becomes the Giver, and the pen is handed to the person on his right, who becomes the Receiver, and so on.

Once the group has successfully passed one object around the circle, and everyone knows the script, the group could try passing two objects. The person with the pen again passes it to the right, and the person on his left hands him a watch at the same time. This means that the person with the pen says both parts of the script — the Giver's and the Receiver's. For example, to the person on the right he'll say, "This is a pen," and then turning to his left, because he's been handed another object, he'll ask, "A what?" and continues both scripts and passes both objects.

The only way to really understand how this game works and how much fun it can be is to try it. Often, someone in the group has played the game and can help move it along.

24. The Minister's Cat

Originally a Victorian parlor game, this warm-up has many variations and is an old standby.

Players sit in a circle on the floor or on chairs. To begin, the first player describes the minister's cat in one sentence using an adjective beginning with "A." For example, "The minister's cat is an angry cat." Each player's adjective must start with a consecutive letter of the alphabet. Thus, the next person in the circle could say, "The minister's cat is a bashful cat," and so on around the circle until the letters in the alphabet have been exhausted. To add more fun and keep the game moving, players could tap a soft rhythm on their knees as they play.

Variation: If the students like the game, they might enjoy a variation. The first player describes the cat with an adjective beginning with "A." Each of the following players in the circle does the same, using different adjectives starting with the same letter until "A" adjectives are exhausted, at which time the players start using "B" adjectives, and so on until the game is over.

25. Clap Out

This game combines math, rhythm, and concentration.

The players stand in a circle. One person is chosen to start by saying, "one." The next person says, "two." The third person claps instead of saying, "three." The next person says, "four," the next says, "five," and the following person claps. Every time a person gets a multiple of three he claps instead of saying the number. A person who says the wrong number, claps at the wrong time, or says the number and claps, is out. Also, if pauses are too long the player is out. When a player gets out, he sits in the middle of the circle.

This warm-up can feel really intimidating at first, so to build confidence, the first few minutes of play could be practice. If time permits, the game could be played until there is only one player remaining.

Variation: Change the numbers and use different multiples.

26. Clap the Ball

A concerted effort to focus and concentrate will ensure success in this challenging warm-up.

Materials: A tennis ball

Players stand in a circle. One person begins by making eye contact with someone across the circle and throws a tennis ball to him. He then throws it to someone else and so on. When the players have become adept at ball tossing, the teacher introduces the idea that everyone claps their hands in unison once while the ball is in the air. If one clap goes well, the game continues so that each time the ball is thrown the group tries to clap together twice. Eventually, the group may even successfully achieve five claps or more.

27. Boingetty

When the pace of play is speeded up in this warm-up, students can practice their ability to focus and speak loudly and crisply.

Players arrange themselves into a standing or sitting circle. The teacher leads the group in the repetition of the following phrase: "Boingetty boing, boingetty boing, boingetty, boingetty, boingetty." To play the game, each player says one word of the phrase at a time. The first player says, "Boingetty," the second says, "boing," and so on around the circle. When the players know the phrase well enough and have become comfortable with the way the phrase moves around the circle, the pace of delivery can be increased and the direction of play can be reversed. If someone hesitates and breaks the rhythm or says the wrong thing, that player sits on the floor inside the circle.

28. Did You Hear?

This game allows actors to practice focusing skills in spite of distractions.

The players are divided into groups of three. While one member of each group counts out loud by fours to one hundred, the other two try to distract him by whispering fairy tales or nursery rhymes in each ear. After the counter reaches one hundred, he tells his partners what tales or nursery rhymes they were saying, and perhaps he could express to his partners what his experience was, what kind of listener he thinks he is, and how he could improve his concentration skills. Group members switch roles so each gets to be the counter.

29. Fuzzy Ducky

Students will run to teach their math teacher this game.

Players stand in a circle. The object is to count clockwise around the circle to a number as high as possible with the following stipulations:

- Any number that is a multiple of three or contains a three, like thirteen, becomes "Fuzzy."
- Any number that is a multiple of seven or contains a seven, like seventeen, becomes "Ducky."
- Any number that is a multiple of three and seven, like twenty-one, or contains both three and seven, like thirty-seven and seventy-three, becomes "Fuzzy Ducky."

For example, the first player would begin by saying one, the second player would say two, the third player would say fuzzy, and so on.

Paying attention is important so that players avoid getting lost or confused.

30. Ha!

This game is a great warm-up to practice focus, and it's amusing to play.

After players are spread out around the room, the game is started with someone shouting, "ha" and then clapping his hands and jumping at the same time. The rest of the players must quickly respond by jumping around to face the person, clapping and saying, "ha." The warm-up continues as random players shout "ha," clap, and jump, and the group responds by imitating. Occasionally, the teacher may need to call out the name of the player to face if more than one person yells "ha."

It's really fun to keep this game moving quickly, and it's important for players not to talk.

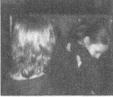

31. Honey, If You Love Me, Smile

This game is one of the best for helping young actors stay in character.

Players form a circle. Choose one player to stay in the center of the circle. One at a time, that player approaches players in the circle and asks, "Honey, do you love me?" The player being questioned must answer, "Honey, I love you, but I just can't smile." If he does smile or laugh, he changes places with the player in the middle. Because they would prefer not to be the person in the middle, players concentrate on remaining stoical. The person in the middle is not allowed to touch other players, but may make funny faces and perform goofy actions in order to make the others smile.

32. I'm Going to Hawaii

This is a wonderful game for cultivating memory and concentration.

Everyone sits in a circle on chairs or on the floor. If the group is large, the players are divided into groups of twelve to fifteen. The first player begins by saying, "I'm going to Hawaii, and I'm taking a basketball (or any other item)." The second player says, "I'm going to Hawaii, and I'm taking a basketball and a laptop." The third player takes a basketball, a laptop, and adds a new item. Each player tries to repeat in exact order the items that were previously mentioned plus a new one. If a player makes a mistake he sits out.

33. Leave Me Alone

This is one of the best warm-ups to test a student's ability to concentrate.

Materials: Index cards, enough lightweight plastic chairs or hula hoops for each group of three to have one

Preparation: Simple addition, subtraction, and multiplication problems, or a combination of the three, are written on index cards.

In a large space, players split up into groups of three. Before the groups begin this warm-up, one group is chosen to demonstrate the way the game works. The teacher tells Actor One that he is going to do some math problems in his head that Actor Two will give him — from the cards that have been handed to him. After Actor One has answered a few problems, the game is made a little more challenging. He is given the plastic chair, and while he is solving the problems he has to hold it in the air by grasping one leg. An alternative to holding the chair would be to spin a hula hoop either on his wrist or around his waist.

While Actor One is attempting to complete his mathematical task while engaging in physical activity, Actor Three asks him questions or carries on a one-sided conversation in an attempt to divert his attention. For example, he could ask "How is your day going?" or "Are you having fun in this moment?" or he could engage in conversation about any topic. Actor One does not have to respond. The three players rotate so everyone has the opportunity of being Actor One.

34. Letter Number Game

Keeping several actions moving around a circle is a good way to challenge the ability to maintain focus.

Everyone sits in a big circle. The teacher begins the game by lifting his right arm in the air and stating his name to the person on his right. The person on the right repeats the same gesture and says his own name. The gesture and name presentation continues around the circle.

After names have progressed to two or three players around the circle, the teacher begins speaking the letters of the alphabet. He "hands" an "a" to the person on his right by raising his right palm outward in a giving gesture. The game is continued with each player repeating the given gesture and saying the next consecutive letter of the alphabet.

After the letters of the alphabet have progressed two or three players around the circle, the same is done with the numbers one through nine, using another gesture, perhaps raising the right foot.

Names, letters of the alphabet, and numbers one through nine make their way around the circle. Success in this game is measured by whether or not the things set in motion by the teacher get back to him.

35. The Lineup

Here is a game that combines focus with cooperation.

Students sit in two or three single file lines facing the teacher. The person at the front of each line engages in simple actions from the waist up so the movement can be seen from behind. The students in the lines concentrate solely on imitating the actions so they appear to be moving in unison. Slow movements could be inspired by listening to a piece of classical music. When everyone is performing in unison, the teacher gives the front person a cue to move to the back of the line, and the

27

next person in line becomes the leader of the movements. After the students have performed actions while sitting down, they could stand up and repeat the process using freer movement involving the whole body.

36. Object Throwaway

It's fun to use this game to practice memory skills and concentration. It's most effective when it moves quickly.

Players stand in three lines — A, B, and C — single file on-stage or in an open area of a classroom. The person at the head of Line A pantomimes using an object such as a bat or flashlight, names it, pantomimes throwing it away, and moves to the back of the line. Then the person at the head of Line B quickly names and mimes a different object, throws it away, and also moves to the back of the line. The first person in Line C does the same. The players who are now at the front of the three lines continue by naming and miming objects, throwing them away, and moving to the back of the line, and so on until the last person in each line is finished. All players watch each other carefully because no one can use an object that has already been thrown away. If a player does, he sits out. Everyone does his best to remain relaxed and focused so he can remember what objects have been thrown out.

37. One Duck

This is one of the very best warm-ups to show the importance of focus, concentration, and memory.

Everyone stands in a circle. Going clockwise around the circle, *one word per person*, the students recite "One duck, two legs, quack. Two ducks, four legs, quack, quack," and so on.

For example:
PLAYER 1: One
PLAYER 2: Duck
PLAYER 3: Two
PLAYER 4: Legs

PLAYER 5: Quack
PLAYER 6: Two
PLAYER 7: Ducks
PLAYER 8: Four
PLAYER 9: Legs
PLAYER 10: Quack
PLAYER 11: Quack

The game continues until someone misses, and then beginning with the person who made the error, everyone starts over with "one."

38. One, Two, Three

Few warm-ups combine the use of focus, memory, and coordination as well as this game.

The group is divided into pairs, facing each other. Each pair starts counting from one to three back and forth between themselves. When one of the partners says "one," he claps his hands. When one of the partners says "three," he bends his knees.

PLAYER 1: One (Claps hands.)
PLAYER 2: Two
PLAYER 1: Three (Bends knees.)
PLAYER 2: One (Claps hands.)
PLAYER 1: Two
PLAYER 2: Three (Bends knees.)

Variation: Played in a circle. Players alternate counting from one to three, and if a player forgets which action to make on a particular number he goes to sit in the center of the circle.

39. One, Two, Three, Four

It's easy to get lost in this warm-up without commitment to staying focused.

This game is a repetition of four movements which the teacher demonstrates:

Touch head with both hands
Touch shoulders with both hands
Touch hips with both hands
Slap right foot with right hand

The challenge is to remain silent on certain numbers while performing a movement only. The players, led by the teacher, repeat the following routine five to ten times. To make it more challenging, the tempo can be increased with each repetition:

- Say one, two, three, four with no movements.
- Touch head on one, but don't say one, and say two, three, four.
- Touch head on one, but don't say one, touch shoulders on two, but don't say two, and say three, four.
- Touch head, touch shoulders, touch hips on one, two, three, but don't say one, two, or three, and say four.
- Touch head, shoulders, hips, slap foot. Don't say anything.

40. Shark

In this game it is crucial to pay attention every moment because it requires quick-wittedness, focus, and concentration.

Players stand in a circle. One player is the shark and stands in the center of the circle with hands clasped together in front of him like the nose of a shark. To begin, the shark silently chooses a victim and walks directly toward one of the players. That player points at someone else in the circle. The person being pointed at shouts out the name of the person pointing before the shark touches him with his clasped hands. If the name is called out correctly before the shark reaches his victim, the shark continues on to his next victim across the circle — not the person standing next to the first victim. If the shark is successful and reaches the victim before the victim's name is called, that player becomes the next shark.

41. Snap Clap

Thinking ahead and participating in rhythm take a coordinated effort.

Players can sit in a circle, but they could also play while sitting in desks or chairs arranged in rows.

A category such as flowers, breeds of dogs, or names of candy bars is chosen. Some time is spent establishing a rhythmical pattern. For example, the students *slap* their thighs or desk, then *clap* their hands, and then *snap* their fingers in a one-two-three rhythm. It's important to keep the rhythm consistent.

On a cue, the game is started by the teacher who leads the rhythm *slap, clap, snap.* On the snap, the teacher says the name of something that fits into the category. The player designated to go next says something else on the next snap and so on until the whole group has contributed an item on the snap.

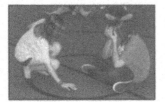

42. Steal the Keys

For an old favorite, this game continues to be a big hit with players. Who doesn't love to be sneaky?

Materials: A ring of keys, blindfold

Players sit on the floor in a large circle with one person blindfolded and sitting in the middle of the circle. A ring of keys is placed in front of him. One person at a time *slowly* sneaks up and quietly attempts to steal the keys. If the person in the middle hears the thief, he points at him, and the thief must go back and sit down, leaving the keys on the floor. The player who succeeds in stealing the keys and returning to his seat without being heard becomes the next person in the middle.

43. Stop, Go, Jump, Clap

Listening skills and concentration are put to the test in this game.

Students spread out so they can move around in a large space. When the teacher calls out "go," they move around the space. They stop when they hear the command to stop. After giving the students the opportunity to practice "stop" and "go" several times, "jump" is called out, and they jump once on the spot and then continue moving. When they hear the command to clap, everyone claps once and continues moving. After the group becomes adept at the commands, it is announced that their meaning will be reversed. "Go" means "stop" and "stop" means "go." Initially, "jump" and "clap" are not reversed, but once the players have gotten good at the original commands, "jump" can become "clap" and "clap" can become "jump." If a player makes a mistake he sits on the sidelines. If time permits, continue play until one person remains.

44. Synchro Clap

This warm-up will completely absorb the whole class.

After everyone is standing in a circle, the group is taught a clapping rhythm that is practiced a few times to make sure the players know the rhythm. Someone starts the game by turning to the person on his right and clapping the rhythm together. The second person immediately turns to his right and engages in the clapping rhythm with the next person, and so on. The object is to stay in rhythm with one's partner and keep the clapping rhythm moving smoothly around the circle until the last person claps it with the person who began. The clapping should be seamless so it is critical that everyone stays focused and ready to clap. To continue the game, ask for volunteers to create new clapping rhythms for the group to synchronize.

45. Two Conversations

A challenging exercise, this game will force the students to be attentive.

The players are split into groups of three. Someone sits in the middle and the other two sit on either side of him. The players on both sides simultaneously hold a conversation with the person in the middle as though there was no one on the other side of him. For example, the person on the middle person's right could engage him in a conversation about last night's football game, while the person on his left dives into a conversation about yesterday's math test. The person in the middle does his best to carry on both conversations. When the time is up, the players rotate.

46. Zip Zap Zoop

Perfect for honing concentration and listening skills, this is a stimulating brain warm-up.

Players form a big circle. The teacher turns to the right, points to the player beside him, and briskly says, "zip." That player has *three* choices: He can turn to the right and say "zip," turn to the person on his left and say "zap," *or* point to someone anywhere across the circle, make eye contact, and say "zoop." If a player is "zooped," his *only* option is to turn to the right and say, "zip". Subsequent players continue to have three choices: zip, zap, or zoop, unless they are "zooped." After the players have had a chance to practice playing for a few minutes, play a round so that when a player makes an incorrect command or is too slow in responding, he sits in the center.

Chapter Four
Getting Ready

*Creativity is inventing, experimenting, growing, taking risks,
breaking rules, making mistakes, and having fun.*
— Mary Lou Cook

For a theatre student, entering a drama class requires a transition from academic classes such as math or science. Before getting ready to take part in activities like scriptwriting or rehearsing a pantomime, it can be helpful to engage in easy and fun physical activities. The purpose of physical warm-ups in a theatre class is to warm up the body, discover and access the creative self, and help release nervous tension — activity eases anxiety.

On a performance day, middle school students bound excitedly into the classroom. One type of warm-up that will help to dissipate some of their nervous energy and alleviate stage fright is a vigorous one. It will help to calm them down and deepen breathing, which is often high and shallow. Any of the warm-ups in this section, sometimes followed by relaxation exercises, help release nervous tension and allow students to relax and be able to focus on their theatrical project.

47. Alien, Tiger, Cow

Somewhat similar to rock, paper, scissors, this game is a fun opportunity to become creature characters!

Everyone forms a large circle. Before the game begins, students learn the gestures and sound effects for each of the three creatures.

Alien: Players hold their index fingers up next to their head as little antennae and say, "bleeb bleeb," bending inward into the circle.

Cow: Players bend forward, hold their right hand on their tummy, and say, "moooo."

Tiger: Players push their hands forward, imitating claws, and roar.

When the teacher signals, every player chooses one of the three creatures to portray. The idea is for everyone to become the same thing, which obviously won't happen on the first attempt because players may not engage in verbal or nonverbal communication. The game could be played until everyone is in sync.

Variation: The class is divided into groups of two to four students. When the teacher signals, each member of the group becomes one of the three creatures with the goal of portraying the same one. There is, of course, a much better chance for the players in the smaller groups of becoming the same creature.

48. Bippety Bop

Quick thinking, reflexes, a cool head, and laughter are the hallmarks of this game.

Players stand in a circle with one player in the middle. The player in the middle closes his eyes, holds his right hand pointing in front of him, and spins around. He stops, opens his eyes, and says as fast as he can, "bippety, bippety, bop." The player to whom he is pointing and the player's two neighbors attempt to build an elephant in less time than the player in the center can say, "bippety, bippety, bop." Any player that cannot get his part accomplished by the time the player in the center of the circle says, "bippety, bippety, bop" takes his place in the center.

Special Instructions

A group of three players create the elephant. The three players stand shoulder to shoulder. The middle player puts one arm straight out in front of him and holds it up with the other hand, while his nose touches the upper part of his straightened arm, making the trunk. The players on his left and right each form an ear, using both arms held in a big circle placed near the middle player's respective ear.

49. Bobs and Statues

This game is simple to play and requires students to pay attention and act quickly.

The students spread out in the playing area and walk fairly briskly without talking. When the teacher calls "bobs," they duck down as quickly as they can, and if they hear "statues," they must quickly freeze. The last student to do the action is out. Play continues until only one student is left.

50. Clumps

After this vigorous game, students will be warmed up and ready for action.

Materials: A CD of lively music

Players spread out in a large space. As soon as they hear the lively music, they begin to move around the room. As the players are moving, the teacher pauses the music and calls out a number. If five is called, for example, they quickly arrange themselves into clumps of five. If there are too few or too many people in a group, the whole group is out. During the warm-up, the players remain spread out at least three feet away from each other. The game can be played until there is only one group of players left.

51. Eights

This exercise is excellent to get muscles warmed up and ready for things theatrical.

Students spread out as the teacher leads them through the following movements:
- Make a figure eight movement with your left big toe, then your left foot, then your whole left leg. Repeat with your right toe, foot, and leg.
- Make a figure eight movement with the index finger of your left hand, then your left hand, then your left arm. Repeat with your right finger, hand, and arm. Then do both arms at the same time.
- Make a figure eight movement with your pelvis. (Be prepared for giggles.)
- Make a figure eight movement with your left then right shoulder, then both shoulders at the same time.
- Make a figure eight movement with your head.

Conclude the exercise by making figure eights simultaneously with as many parts of your body as possible.

52. Elbow, Fruit, Hop

*When this game moves quickly
it's an excellent workout.*

Players stand next to their desks or chairs or in a large open space. At the front of the room the teacher rings a bell or shakes a noisemaker and then names three things. The first thing is a part of the body for the players to touch — like the elbow. The second is a category from which the players can each choose one item — like fruit, cars, birds. The third is a way for players to move — like hop or walk backwards.

For example, if a player calls out "head, chocolate bar, skip," everyone would skip around touching their heads and calling out the name of a chocolate bar until someone takes the initiative to run to the front of the room, ring the bell, and call out three different items, like "wrist, flower, crawl."

This game is best when it moves quickly. Students may need encouragement to volunteer to ring the bell. To end the fun, the teacher blows the whistle and calls "elbow, fruit, hop."

53. Energy 1-10

*This game warms a group up in
a very short time.*

After students get into a big circle, they squat down. On cue, everyone counts from one to ten in unison. As each number is counted, the students slowly move up, with increasing energy and volume, to a standing position. One is barely audible with everyone squatting. Ten is as loud and vigorous as possible with everyone standing up straight and arms high in the air. Students watch each other and listen carefully, making sure everyone is at the same height and volume.

54. Fruit Salad

Players will enjoy the movement inherent in this fun version of musical chairs.

Players sit in a circle with one less chair than the number of players. The teacher stands in the middle of the circle and has the players count off, "apple, banana, orange, apple, banana, orange" around the circle. When the teacher calls out one or more of the three fruits, all those designated players must get up and change places at least two seats away from where they're sitting, and the teacher tries to find a vacant seat. When the teacher succeeds in finding a place to sit, the player who remains standing takes the center of the circle. His goal and the goal of all subsequent callers is to find a place to sit when players move. Whenever the caller yells "fruit salad" everyone gets up and changes places. The player left without a seat becomes the caller.

55. Grandmother's Footsteps

This game is similar to the children's game, What's the Time, Mister Wolf? and requires a large playing space.

Someone is asked to play Grandmother, who stands at one end of the room, facing away from the other players standing at the opposite end, at least twenty feet away. On a cue, the players quietly start moving toward Grandmother. Whenever she turns around, the players must stop moving immediately. If Granny sees anyone moving, she sends them back to the starting point, and they have to start all over again. The first player to tap Grandmother on the shoulder is the winner.

56. Ho!

Play this game when students seem tired or listless.

Players stand in a big circle. One person is selected to start. He then runs across the circle and approaches another player. Together, the two players jump in the air, clap their hands in a high five, and say, "Ho!" Then they switch places.

The second player then runs up to another player, they clap hands, and yell, "Ho!" The game continues until all players have had a chance to yell, "Ho!"

Variation: More than one player runs across the circle and yells, "Ho!"

57. Jumpers

Another energetic warm-up and a sure-fire cure for lethargy.

The teacher and students all stand facing the front of the room. On cue, everyone jumps up and down four times facing the front of the room, four times facing the right side of the room, four times facing the back, and four times facing the left side of the room. Then, they jump three times facing the front, three times right, three times to the back, and three to the left. Then the students jump two times facing the front, right, back, then left. Finally, they finish with one time in the four directions. To facilitate jumping together, everyone calls the numbers out loud.

To prevent dizziness, the players could change directions and turn left instead of right as the number of jumps decreases.

58. Kitty Wants a Corner

Here is one variation of an old game.

Players stand in a large circle. The teacher chooses someone to be Kitty, who doesn't have a place to live. This game is about Kitty finding an open spot in the circle.

To begin, Kitty stands in the center of the circle and then walks up to a person in the circle and says, "Kitty wants a corner." That person points to someone else in the circle and says, "Go ask my neighbor." Kitty then goes to that player and says, "Kitty wants a corner."

The fun part of the game is that, while Kitty is approaching people in the circle, players try to switch places by signaling each other, preferably with eye contact, so that Kitty can't see what they're doing. At any time, Kitty can steal an open space left by others in the circle. The person left without a space becomes Kitty, and the game continues.

59. Leading

Players enjoy following the instruction in this game and being a little silly.

The players spread out in an open space. The teacher calls out a body part with which the students can lead their body. For example, "Everyone move around as if your nose were leading you." Students move with their nose leading for about thirty seconds, making sure to stay spread out. Other students are then welcome at any time to call out body parts with which to lead their bodies: knee, derrière, left foot, right ear, tummy, and so on. Play can continue until students run out of appropriate body parts.

60. Lemonade

Don't be afraid to try this brisk warm-up that needs a large space. Instead of acting out a word or phrase, players act out occupations.

Players are divided into two groups who stand in parallel lines, about fifteen feet apart, facing each other.

Each group gets into a huddle behind their line to decide what occupation they will act out, and it is decided which team will begin. The teams take part in the following chant:

GROUP 1: Where are you from? (The line takes two short stomping steps forward.)

GROUP 2: New York! (Or anywhere. The line takes two short stomping steps forward.)

GROUP 1: What's your trade? (The line takes two short stomping steps forward.)

GROUP 2: Lemonade. (The line takes two short stomping steps forward.)

GROUP 1: Give us some if you're not afraid!

At the end of the chant, the teams should be about eight feet apart. After they shout, "Give us some if you're not afraid," each member of Group 2 mimes the profession and Group 1 tries to guess it. When someone from Group 1 correctly guesses the profession, members of Group 2 turn and run back toward their starting line while being chased by members of Group 1 who try to tag them, but once they cross the starting line, they are safe. Those who are tagged join the opposing team. The second team then chooses a trade among themselves and the game is repeated.

Before the game begins, the number of turns for each team is established. At the end of the last "inning," the team with the most players wins.

61. Loosey Goosey

This energizing warm-up helps to loosen all the joints of the body.

Everyone stands up and spreads out so they have space to move. The following instructions are given by the teacher:

- Hold both your arms straight out in front of you. From your wrists, make circles, right hand turning to the right, left to the left. Do that five times. Now turn to the left five times.
- Now, make big circles with both arms. Forward five times. Now back five times.
- Now, standing on your left foot, raise your right leg a bit off the floor and make circles to the right with your foot. Five circles to the right. Now five to the left. Let's do the same with our left foot. Five circles to the right. Five to the left.
- Standing on your left leg, raise your right knee high. Make circles going outward with your right leg from the knee down. Five circles to the right. Five to the left. Repeat with the left leg, standing on your right. Five circles to the right. Five to the left.
- Now, put your hands on your hips. Make large circles with your whole upper body, pivoting from the waist. First to the right five times. Reverse. Circle to the left five times.
- Gently roll your head in circles to the right five times. To the left five times.
- Shake your whole body from head to toe. Relax and sit.

62. Man Overboard

Players of any age enjoy the movement and competition in this game.

Players spread out in the room like an aerobics class. The teacher pretends to be the captain of a ship and calls out commands. It is important to establish which side of the room is the bow of the ship and to review the other three sides: stern, starboard, port. The bow could be assigned to the area where the teacher is standing. Before beginning the game, the group practices the following commands:

Bow – all run to the front of the playing space
Stern – all run to the back of the playing space
Starboard – all run to the right of the playing space
Port – all run to the left of the playing space
Hit the deck – lie face down on the floor
Captain is coming – stand at attention and salute
Man overboard – grab a partner
Man the lifeboats – get into a group of two pairs and start rowing
Sharks – get off the ground somehow

After each command, a player who is too slow or does the wrong action sits out. The last player to remain in the game is declared the winner.

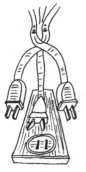

63. Mr. Electricity

This warm-up is a humorous and effective way to get students moving.

Players stand in a circle. Mr. Electricity, an imaginary blob of energy, is jumpy and whatever part of the body he touches, shakes. He is tossed around the circle and each player catches him on a different part of his body. The teacher starts, perhaps by having Mr. Electricity in his hand, which is shaking. He makes eye contact with another student in the circle and tosses Mr. Electricity to him. That person could catch Mr. Electricity on his foot, and his foot shakes, and so on. Play the game until each player has caught Mr. Electricity and is "all shook up."

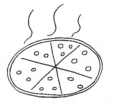

64. People Who ...

Once students have played this game, they clamor to play it again. It's a fast-paced, aerobic activity.

Everyone sits on chairs in a large circle, with the teacher standing in the middle so there is one more player than there are chairs. The teacher begins by saying, "I like people who are wearing blue," or "I like people who like pizza," or any other statement that describes as many students as possible because the objective of the person in the middle is to find a place to sit. Anyone who is described by the statement gets up and moves quickly to switch chairs with the other people who have also risen. Everyone must move at least two chairs away from where they were sitting. Whoever is left standing remains in the middle and makes another describing statement.

Chapter Five
Improvisation

"Everyone can act. Everyone can improvise.
Anyone who wishes to can play in the theater ... "
— Viola Spolin

Like most theatre arts, improvisational theatre has a colorful past. Its oldest ancestor may be Commedia dell'Arte, which was popular during the Renaissance. Troupes of actors would travel from town to town performing plays improvised from rough plot outlines.

It took nearly 500 years for the next innovations to occur. The following innovators are revered by teachers of improvisation: Viola Spolin was the earliest practitioner and her book, *Improvisation for the Theatre*, is a dog-eared volume on theatre teachers' book shelves; Del Close was an influential director associated with the Chicago improvisation movement; Keith Johnstone is a teacher who invented many games and exercises that have become classics.

Improvisation is the performance of a scene by actors who have had little or no advance preparation. The opportunity to improvise either strikes fear or elicits excitement in the hearts of young actors. Many who are familiar with the performances of seasoned actors on *Whose Line Is It, Anyway?* or in a *Comedy Sportz* performance have the impression that doing improv is easy, and for a few, perhaps it is. Doing it well, however, takes courage, quick wit, and the willingness to take a risk.

Although improvisation often requires years to master, giving students the opportunity to experience improv builds self-confidence. When actors are given the opportunity to create a scene without a script, they amass successful experiences in adapting to new situations and becoming flexible and creative when put on the spot. They build "quick thinking muscles." In an impromptu setting they can revel in their growing skill at creating something out of nothing.

Improvisation helps to improve speaking and listening skills. After experiences in improv, actors realize that it is not a threatening experience because they learn to relax and trust themselves to be able to come up with thoughts quickly and express themselves cleverly. They are forced to listen because they don't know what another actor is going to say. They begin to understand the importance of listening with intention and work at being present in the moment so they hear what their fellow actors say and can respond intelligently and believably.

Improv also fosters cooperation. When actors work together in an unrehearsed scene they are focused on a mutual goal. Therefore, they are not solo actors; they learn to listen carefully to each other and work together as a creative team.

Improv provides opportunities for creativity. When actors have no script and receive only a rough description of character and/or plot, they are forced to visualize their own character, create their own plot, and make up their own dialogue. For young theatre students, improvising is not easy, but they are usually willing to take risks and are eager for new experiences.

In my middle school theatre classes, I usually save improvisation for the end of a semester when students have chalked up hours of experience on-stage working in scripted and non-scripted performances. The warm-ups in this section will help prepare students for a more in-depth experience of improv.

65. A Story to Tell

Performing improv requires quick thinking, and this warm-up will involve students in the creation of a sometimes strange, speedily created story.

Materials: Kitchen timer

Students stand or sit in a circle. The teacher moves around the circle whispering the name of a person, place, or thing to each player. A player is chosen or volunteers to begin telling an original story, and the teacher sets a timer for ten seconds. Within ten seconds, the storyteller must mention the person, place, or thing that was assigned to him. When the timer goes off, the next person in the circle continues telling the story, making sure to mention his assigned person, place, or thing within ten seconds. The game is played until all players have had the opportunity to add to the story.

66. Character Walks

An actor takes great care to make a character physically believable. This warm-up allows students to practice a character's walk.

Students stand in a circle. They then begin walking in one direction together in a circle. As the teacher calls out commands, the students change the way they walk. For example, the teacher could say, "Walk like you just received an A on your math test," or "Walk like you are an ugly green monster."

Walks
An old person
A movie star
A football player
A burglar
A little girl who has lost her dog
A clown

67. Emotions Characters

This is a warm-up to give students practice in making emotions convincing.

Students are arranged in pairs facing each other. They are instructed to look at each other with pity. They may not speak or make sounds or use their hands. Then everyone finds a new partner somewhere else in the room, and the players look at each other fearfully. Everyone then changes partners again and looks at each other joyfully. Then each one of the three emotions is called out again, one at a time, and players must find the partner with whom they acted out that emotion the first time and share the expression again.

Now, have the players quietly walk around the room and maintain neutral expressions. When they meet one of their three partners, they emulate the look that went with the emotion they shared with that partner. The teacher does not call out the expressions at this point.

Many other emotions can be substituted for or added to pity, fear, and joy.

68. Emotional Mirror

This game can provide an intense experience using emotions.

Materials: White board and markers

Preparation: Players brainstorm a list of emotions while the teacher writes them on the board.

The players are arranged in pairs, facing each other. One member of a pair chooses an emotion, shares it with his partner, and then starts to talk in gibberish, as a way of expressing the emotion. His partner mimics the emotion by speaking in his own gibberish to express it. Both players keep talking. No pauses allowed! After about ten seconds, the second member of the pair chooses a different emotion, talks in gibberish, and his partner follows suit. Each pair could continue this exercise by expressing four or five emotions.

69. Exaggeration Circle

An excellent warm-up, this game provides practice using gestures.

The class is split into groups of eight to ten. Each group forms a circle. One student in each group makes a little gesture with a soft sound. The student to the right imitates the gesture and sound, but makes it just a little bigger and louder. Each consecutive player makes the gesture and sound just a bit bigger and louder than the player before. The last player does the gesture and sound to the extreme, and the exaggeration circle is complete.

70. Free Association

Students love this quick-thinking exercise.

Players stand in a circle. One person starts by saying any word, such as "snow." The person to his left quickly says the first word that comes to mind, like "rain," and the next person might say "storm." Each person continues to make free associations with the word they receive and so on around the circle until everyone has made an association. The emphasis is on quick association!

71. Gibberish Dictionary

This game is an opportunity for students to use their imagination quickly and have some fun creating clever definitions.

Students stand in a circle. One person turns to the person on his right and says a gibberish word — a nonsense word not found in the dictionary — like "kabluk." That student repeats the word and makes up a definition for it, perhaps "a puddle found under the swings in a park," or "a tool used to raise a window that's stuck." He then turns to the person to his right and says a new gibberish word. Gibberish words and definitions move around the circle until the first person who gave a gibberish word concludes the warm-up with a definition for the word given from the person on his left.

72. Greetings

Although somewhat stereotypical, the aspects of character brought out in this warm-up could lead to something more believable.

Everyone starts to mill around the room. The teacher calls out ways for players to greet each other. For example, if the teacher calls out "business-like," they could simply shake hands. They then move to somewhere else in the room and are instructed to greet the next player they meet in a new way.

Ways to Greet
Long-lost friends
Clowns
Cowboys
Someone you have a secret crush on
Old person
Someone who has just gotten out of bed
Someone you don't really trust

73. Honey Walk

In this warm-up the students are reminded that they can more effectively remember things they've experienced through their sense of touch.

Students spread throughout the playing area. As the teacher leads them through the exercise, they imagine that they are wearing an oxygen mask and pretend to move through the space in successively thicker substances. They are prompted to imagine really moving through the following substances, feeling them on their hands, in their hair, and all over their bodies.

Mist
Warm water
Olive oil
Honey
Jell-o
Syrup
Wet cement

The game ends with the students imagining that they are frozen in cement, and on cue they forcefully and loudly break out.

74. The Machine

This is a great add-on game.

The group is divided in half. One half is chosen to create a machine. The first player enters the playing area and begins making a repetitive sound, such as "beep, beep, beep," and a motion that goes with it, like pushing a button. The next player steps into the playing area and makes a different repetitive sound and motion that connects to the machine by making physical contact with the first person. Each new machine part may connect to any other by using an arm, finger, elbow, foot, or other body part. Players should be reminded to make appropriate contact when they connect to the machine. The game continues as players add themselves one at a time to the machine until everyone is part of it. The warm-up continues with the other half of the class creating a separate machine. It is fun to have the teams come up with a name for the machines they've created.

75. Presents

This game is most enjoyable when it moves quickly so players don't have much time to think about what gift they've just received.

Players choose a partner. The pairs stand facing each other. Each partner gives the other an imaginary present. The Giver pantomimes picking up the present from a table or from the floor. He then hands the gift to the Receiver. Upon accepting the present, the Receiver gives the gift a name, even though he has no idea what it is. For example, he might say, "Oh, thanks for the inner tube." He is then the Giver and pantomimes placing the gift aside and turns to his partner, picks up a gift, hands it to him, and the Receiver names the gift and expresses thanks.

76. The Story

For a wonderful twist on storytelling, this improv game will provide an experience in quick, creative thinking.

Preparation: Index cards are cut in half and the name of a person, place, or thing is written on each.

Players stand or sit in a circle. The teacher walks around the circle and hands a card to each player. For example, a player could be handed a card with "pirate" written on it. One person in the group has ten seconds to begin telling an original story using whatever word is written on his card. Then the next player must weave into the story the person, place, or thing he has been assigned, and so on. The storytelling continues around the circle until everyone has had a turn. Stories can get a bit strange, but that's part of the fun.

77. Story Orchestra

Students enjoy taking part in this unique orchestra.

Preparation: The teacher compiles background information on the elements of a good story to share with the students before they play the game.

The students sit at their desks, in chairs, or on the floor facing the teacher who pretends to conduct a storytelling orchestra. A student is chosen to begin the story. From then on, the students tell a story as the conductor points to them one at a time. A storyteller may be interrupted at any time, even in the middle of a sentence, and a new player is chosen to continue telling the story. The conductor can continue in that role until the story is told, or guest conductors can be chosen to fill in at any time in the storytelling presentation. The story orchestra performs until the story reaches a satisfactory conclusion or time runs out.

78. Story Story

A clever game, this warm-up is an absorbing combination of pantomime and improv storytelling.

Students sit in a semi-circle around the acting area. The leader establishes an order of play so everyone will know whose turn it is. Player A stands in the acting area. Player B stands stage right of Player A and begins to tell a story. Player A acts out the story in pantomime in as much detail as possible.

After a minute or so, a signal is given for Player A to sit down. Player B moves into the acting position. A new player comes on-stage, stands stage right of Player B, and continues the story where it left off. Again, after a minute or so, a signal is given and players rotate. Rotations continue until the story ends or seems to peter out or until everyone has had several turns as storyteller and as actor.

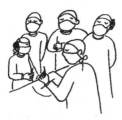

79. Who Am I?

This is a good large group improv warm-up.

There is no special seating arrangement for this game. One student, Player 1, leaves the room. The teacher and the rest of the group choose the setting of the scene that will be acted out, the role that each of the players will take, and the character that Player 1 will portray. It works best for Player 1 to be one who is involved in a lot of activity. For example, he could be a news reporter in a studio or news room, a traffic cop, or the coach of a little league team.

The group begins acting out the activity, and the teacher asks Player 1 to return. The other players should immediately involve the first player in what is happening. Player 1 tries to guess the role he thinks he's playing and the setting he is involved in. The same process can then be repeated in a new setting with a different student.

80. Word at a Time Story

This engaging warm-up is wonderful for stimulating imagination, encouraging quick thinking, and fostering good listening and focusing skills.

Students stand or sit in a circle. The teacher reminds the students that a story needs a main character, a beginning, middle, and end, and it must come to a satisfying conclusion. The students tell a story by each offering *one* word at a time around the circle. The first word can be offered by the teacher or a student. The next person in the circle offers the next word and so on around the circle. Be ready for some unusual characters, plots, and endings. Occasionally, it might be necessary for the teacher to prompt the students to keep the story moving.

81. Word Ball

Students remember this warm-up and ask to play it again and again.

Materials: A small, lightweight ball

Students stand in a circle. The student who is chosen to begin makes eye contact with someone else across the circle and tosses a lightweight ball to him while saying a word, such as "squirrel." The person who receives the ball makes eye contact with another student across the circle and, while throwing the ball, says a word that is associated with the first word, such as "tree." The game continues until everyone has thrown the ball and made an association.

Chapter Six
Listening

"To listen well is as powerful a means of influence as to talk well, and is as essential to all true conversation."
— Chinese Proverb

Robert Lewis, the well-known director and author, said "Listen for clues, for the ways a speaker feels, for the truth of what is being said, for what is missed, for what to answer ... " Being able to listen well is a necessary skill for an actor. On-stage, in order to make characters seem real, actors must respond to each other in a believable way. They must pay attention to each other and interact as if they really are the characters they are playing. Actors cannot reply appropriately if they aren't listening to each other. A scene between two or more actors doesn't make sense unless the actors hear their partners so they know how to respond believably.

For an actor, listening goes hand in hand with concentration. In order to hear what a character is saying, an actor must have strong, well-developed concentration skills. When an actor is aware of, but has the ability to block out distractions — the audience, backstage sounds, an uncomfortable costume — he is capable of listening and reacting as his character would.

Listening is an active art and a skill that can be developed and refined. The following warm-ups give students opportunities to focus in order to block out distractions and to learn to listen successfully.

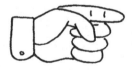

82. Bing Bang Bong

This game is similar to Zip Zap Zoop, but uses different words. It's great to help develop focus, concentration, and memory skills.

The players stand in a close circle so their elbows are nearly touching. This game is more challenging if it is played at a rapid pace. To start the game, a player puts his hands together and points toward any person in the circle except the person to his immediate right or left. As he points, he says, "bing." That person points to someone else in the circle and says, "bang." Finally, the third person points to someone and says, "bong." The game continues with players repeating and passing "bing, bang, bong" back and forth across the circle.

When players become adept at this warm-up, making a mistake results in being sent to sit in the center of the circle. For example, if someone points to Jim and says "bing" and Jim says "bing" to the next person, Jim is out. Or, if John freezes and says nothing, he is out. If time permits, play can continue until one person is left standing.

83. Find the Sound, Feel the Hand

This exercise is a valuable warm-up to improve listening and observation skills.

Students are split into pairs and turn to face each other. They hold hands and take turns making a sound that is easily repeated. As they hold hands they focus on what each other's hand feels like so that later they can remember the touch. After partners have shared sounds while holding hands, they close their eyes and walk slowly around the room making their noise. The goal for everyone is to find their partner. If a student is unsure a person's sound is that of his partner, he can hold the student's hand to make positive identification.

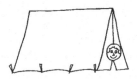

84. Flee Fly Flo

Derived from an old summer camp chant, this version is great fun and helps to exercise listening skills.

This game can be played with the players in a circle or in a typical classroom seating arrangement. The teacher says a line and the students echo:

TEACHER: Flee.
STUDENTS: Flee.
TEACHER: Flee fly.
STUDENTS: Flee fly.
TEACHER: Cooma la.
STUDENTS: Cooma la.
TEACHER: Cooma la, cooma la, cooma la veesta.
STUDENTS: Cooma la, cooma la, cooma la veesta.

TEACHER: No, no, no, no, not the veesta.
STUDENTS: No, no, no, no, not the veesta.
TEACHER: Eenie meenie deci meenie, ooh ah ooh ah la meenie.
STUDENTS: Eenie meenie deci meenie, ooh ah ooh ah la meenie.
TEACHER: Exa meenie zala meenie, ooh ah ooh ah.
STUDENTS: Exa meenie zala, meenie ooh ah ooh ah.
TEACHER: Beep Billy oaten doaten, bo bo ba deeten dahten.
STUDENTS: Beep Billy oaten doaten, bo bo ba deeten dahten.
TEACHER: Shhhh!
STUDENTS: Shhhh!

Variation: A student leads the chant.

85. Fortunately/Unfortunately

Telling a group story requires students to use their imagination and to listen carefully to fellow storytellers.

Preparation: The teacher and students brainstorm titles for a story the group is going to tell.

Students sit or stand in a circle and choose a story title from the list. One person is chosen to begin, and based on the title the group has chosen, starts telling a story. The second person continues the story beginning with "fortunately." The third person continues telling the story beginning with "unfortunately." Each storyteller takes about ten seconds to relate his part of the story. The story moves around the circle alternating between fortunate and unfortunate aspects until everyone has contributed and/or the story reaches a satisfying ending.

For example, if the group chooses to tell a story entitled *The New Bicycle,* the first person could begin by saying, "This summer was the best one ever. For my birthday, I got a new bicycle." The next person could say, "Fortunately, I had lots of time to ride it." The next person could add, "Unfortunately, my mother made me find a job." And the story continues.

86. Gossip

There is nothing like the old parlor game of Gossip *to practice good listening skills.*

Materials: Index cards, a basket

Preparations: The teacher and/or students write unusual messages on index cards and then put them in the basket.

The class is divided into groups of six to eight students who sit or stand in single file. The person at the front of the line picks a message from the basket and *whispers* it to the person next in line, who then *whispers* it to the next person, and so on. Players aren't allowed to repeat the message. If someone doesn't quite hear the sentence or doesn't quite understand it, he tells the next person what he thinks was said. The last person in each line shares the message he received with the whole class. The group that successfully passes the original message or comes the closest to the beginning message is the winner.

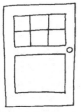

87. Knocking

This is a unique way of incorporating an opportunity to listen and to exercise sensory recall.

Players sit in their usual classroom arrangement. They have their eyes closed while the teacher knocks distinctly three times on any object in the room, and then walks noiselessly away from it. The players are told when to open their eyes and identify the object that was knocked upon. If no one identifies the object, the players again close their eyes, and the teacher repeats the knocking on the same object. Knocking can be performed on several objects.

At the end of the warm-up, a discussion of how the players were able to distinguish the objects knocked upon could be conducted. Some questions that could be asked are: Does wood sound different from metal? Does a wall sound different from a desk? Why?

88. Listen to the Birdie

This game is a good one for developing sensory awareness, but it also helps to develop the ability to concentrate and remember details.

Before beginning this warm-up, the classroom doors and windows are opened. Students sit in their usual seating arrangement. They are asked to close their eyes and remain quiet for a minute so they can listen and remember the sounds they hear in the classroom and outdoors. After the students have listened to the sounds in their environment, they list the sounds they heard and then share them with the rest of the group.

Variation: The teacher is concealed behind a screen, wall, or door and creates noises for the class to identify i.e., keys jangling, coins jingling, a cork popping, and other unique sounds. To extend the game further, students could one at a time conceal themselves and create sounds for their classmates to distinguish.

89. Overload

This game is an excellent exercise to help improve listening skills and concentration by means of sensory overload.

Players are divided into groups of four. One is chosen to be in the "hot seat" with one player standing on his left, one on his right, and one in front of him. He is bombarded with the following stimuli: The player on his left asks him a simple math question, the player on his right asks him a simple personal question, the player in front of him demands that he mirror simple movements.

If the player in the "hot seat" misses something or fails to answer a question or mirror movements, the player who has not been responded to keeps saying, "beep, beep, beep" until the question is answered or the movement is mirrored.

Players rotate after a few minutes so everyone gets an opportunity to experience sensory overload.

90. Question Game

Although essentially a listening game, this warm-up combines paying attention with remembering instructions.

The students must know each other's names to play this game.

The students sit in a circle. If a group is large, the students could be divided into two or more circles. One person in the circle begins by addressing another student by name and asking him a question. The person must respond with the questioner's name and then answer the question with another question.

Example:
JOHN: Sarah, why is the sky blue?
SARAH: Joe, what is your dog's name?
JOE: Allen, did your team win yesterday?

When a student answers a question instead of asking a question or can't think of a question to ask someone else, he moves to the center of the circle. The more quickly the questions are asked, the more fun the game becomes. Play continues until everyone has had a chance to ask a question.

91. Singing Syllables

This warm-up will certainly provide a listening challenge.

Players stand in a circle. One player volunteers or is appointed to leave the room. The remaining players choose a word that has at least three syllables, i.e., auditorium. The players are then divided into the same number of groups as there are syllables contained in the word they've chosen. For auditorium, the players would be divided into five groups. The syllables of the word are distributed around the groups: "au" is given to the first group, "di" to the second group, "to" to the third group, "ri" to the fourth group, and "um" to the fifth group. The groups sing their syllable over and over simultaneously to a familiar tune, like *Yankee Doodle*. The player who was asked to leave the room returns and walks around from group to group and tries to piece the word together, using as many guesses as needed.

92. Talk Fest

Discussion after this warm-up will remind young actors how to be good listeners.

The group is divided in half. The students line up in two rows, standing back to back. At a signal from the teacher, the players turn around quickly and face their partners. They talk to each other at the same time about anything at all without stopping for thirty seconds. What they say doesn't have to make sense.

A discussion after the talk fest could be stimulating. How did the players feel about talking continuously and not listening to their partner? Was it easy to talk non-stop? Did they hear anything their partner said? Did they want to stop talking? What is the purpose of this warm-up?

Variation: The game can be played with only two players talking at a time. They stand in the middle of the room talking fast and continuously while the rest of the players watch. A contest can be set up, and those receiving the most applause are the winners.

93. Traffic Lights

A simple version of Simon Says, *this warm-up quickly provides an opportunity to focus and listen well.*

In a large open space, students stand in a line, facing the teacher who is standing about twenty feet away. They must move according to the following code when the teacher calls out the colors of the traffic light: green means take one step forward, red means take one step backward, yellow means don't move. The last student to follow each instruction or to do the wrong thing sits out.

94. Up, Down, Freeze

This game was created for young children but works well as a listening warm-up for any age group.

The teacher demonstrates the commands that will be used for the game. The students then walk quietly around the playing area. When the teacher gives a command, the students freeze in the position called out by the teacher. Anyone who performs the wrong command, reacts too slowly, or does not freeze sits out.

Commands:
Up – hands in the air
Down – drop to the ground
Heads – hands on head
Shoulders – hands on shoulders
One Leg – stand still with one leg in the air

Chapter Seven
Name Games and Getting to Know You

"Getting to know you, getting to know all about you ... "
— *Oscar Hammerstein*

Students often enter a new class with feelings of anxiety. Used on the first day or during the first week of class, games offer a light-hearted beginning, help to relax initial social anxieties, and allow students to begin to make new acquaintances. In any class where students have come together for the first time, it is important to give them an informal, non-threatening opportunity to get to know each other.

In a theatre class, students spend a lot of time brainstorming, rehearsing, and performing together. It helps to make performances and projects run smoothly when they have many varied experiences together. These types of activities can also be a boon to teachers because names can be learned easily and quickly, potential class leaders revealed, and skills and talents possessed by students are drawn out.

95. Alliteration Introduction

This is one of many delightful name games to help students and teacher get to know each other quickly.

Everyone stands in a circle. One player starts the game by combining an alliterative adjective with his first name. For example, "I'm Smart Steve." The next player introduces the first player and then introduces himself using alliteration. For example, "This is Smart Steve, and I'm Athletic Aaron." Introductions continue around the circle two people at a time. For example, the next person in the circle might say, "This is Athletic Aaron, and I'm Musical Max." After everyone has been introduced, the teacher can move around the circle pointing to various students and asking the others to name him.

96. Animal Groups

Students enjoy moving around the room in this excellent icebreaker.

This warm-up works best in a large, empty space. Each student is assigned to be one of five farm animals. The players then scatter themselves around the room. The teacher turns out the lights or has everyone close their eyes. On cue, the players make the sound of the animal they've been assigned and move around the room listening for other members of their group. When students find the other members of their group, they introduce themselves and share three interesting details about their lives.

97. Autographs

This is a unique way to match faces to names.

Preparation: A sheet is created that has the students' names alphabetized and a blank space after each name with room for a signature.

The teacher gives the students a copy of the class list and then everyone goes around the room matching students with the correct names on the list. They ask their new acquaintance to put their autograph in the appropriate space. It's important that students make a point of looking closely at each other and perhaps having a short conversation so that they can remember each other's name.

After the students have everyone's autograph, they could take part in a contest to prove that they have made new acquaintances. For example, the teacher could randomly choose ten students to stand at the front of the room. The rest of the students number a piece of paper from one to ten. Then, one at a time, the teacher points to the ten students. Their new classmates do their best to write the names of the students on their piece of paper. The person who gets the most names correct is the winner and receives praise for being an observant player.

98. Birthdays

This game gives students a chance to get to know each other by working together for the first time.

Students stand throughout the room. On the teacher's cue, the players quickly form groups of the same birthday months. For example, all those with January birthdays will be in the same group. When the groups are formed, the teacher calls out each month to be sure that everyone is in the right group.

Next, the groups will have ten minutes to create and rehearse a group cheer with movement and hand motions for their month. It might be helpful to give an example, "May, May, whaddaya say? We're *the* month so get outa our way," and give sample motions to go with the cheer. If there is only one student with a birthday in a certain month, that person could work with another group and they could do a cheer incorporating both months.

After the cheers have been created and rehearsed, everyone sits down with their group, facing the stage or the open end of a semicircle. Each month performs their cheer for the other months, in order. As soon as December has performed their cheer, everyone gets to their feet and gives each other a standing ovation.

99. Catch My Name

In this game alertness and eye contact are important to learning names.

Materials: A small beanbag or medium-sized playground ball

The group stands in a circle. A player begins by making eye contact with another player across the circle, throws the object, and says, "Hi, I'm (insert name)." The player who receives the object makes eye contact with someone else across the circle, throws, and says, "Hi, my name is (insert name)." The teacher makes sure that everyone has a turn.

Variation: A player says his name and the name of the person he is throwing to, "Jeremy to Kevin."

100. Clocks

This activity presents many delightful possibilities. It can be utilized any time a teacher wants students to get to know each other better or wants them to engage in thought-provoking discussion and make some observations about what they've learned.

Materials: Small bell, chime, or something else to indicate time is up

On an 8 1/2" by 11" sheet of notebook paper, each student draws a clock face and labels it with numbers, but no hands.

The first step is to have the students move around the room making appointments with each other, preferably with those they don't know very well. For example, "Do you have a one o'clock appointment? You do? Well, let's meet at one o'clock." Then they write each other's names at one on their clock. Or, another example, "Oh, you already have a one o'clock appointment? Then how about meeting with me at three o'clock?" When everyone has filled their clock faces by writing a name next to each time, they fulfill the meetings with their appointments. Give the students a topic to discuss with each other for thirty seconds at each of their appointments, starting with their twelve o'clock appointment. For example, at their twelve o'clock appointment, they could talk about why they signed up for theatre class. After thirty seconds, the teacher rings a small bell to get the students' attention, tells them their next topic, and sends them to meet their one o'clock appointment.

Topics

What comes to mind when you hear the word drama or theatre?
Who is your favorite actor or actress?
Describe the things that you do well.
What do you like best about school?

The possibilities are limitless.

101. Get It Together

This is my favorite way to encourage students to meet someone new. The purpose for this warm-up is to get students interacting.

Have the students line up or get in groups according to a prescribed order. They must communicate well and pay attention to accomplish this.

Orders or Groups

Line up alphabetically by last name.
Line up alphabetically by mother's or father's first name.
Line up in order of birth months, January to December.
Gather into groups according to the color of their shirt.
Gather into groups according to the number of brothers
 and sisters they have.
Gather into groups according to their favorite ice cream flavor.

102. Hey, Hey, Who's in Town?

Students can learn through repetition, so this warm-up is an excellent way to learn names. It alternates between a group chant and a chant by each of three students introducing themselves.

Students sit in a circle on the floor. Before beginning the activity, students count to three around the circle to form groups of three.

Everyone learns the following chant that is accompanied with a clapping rhythm by clapping on the italicized words:

Hey, hey, *who's* in town?
Every body take a *look* around.
Say your name and *when* you do
We will say it *back* to you.

To begin, everyone voices the chant, and then the first three students chant their names, one at a time, and the remainder of the group repeats each name:

STUDENT 1: I am Alex.
GROUP: You are Alex.
STUDENT 2: I am Joseph.
GROUP: You are Joseph.
STUDENT 3: I am Steven.
GROUP: You are Steven.

Then everyone voices the chant again and the next three students chant their names, and so on around the circle until everyone has had a turn.

103. Hi, I'm Bob from Boston

This warm-up is an imaginative way for a group to get to know each others' names.

The class stands in a circle. One person introduces himself by first name and then names a city that starts with the same first letter. For example, "Hi, I'm Bob from Boston." The next person introduces the first person, and then introduces himself using his first name and a city that starts with the first letter of his name. For example, "This is Bob from Boston, and I'm Sean from San Francisco." The students continue around the circle, naming the student before them and introducing themselves.

Variation: Have the students name everyone who preceded them in the circle, and then themselves. The last person would name everyone.

Hello, my name is

104. Name Exchange

Students will enjoy this surefire way to meet at least one new person.

Preparation: The teacher makes a name tag for each student, or the students make their own and give it to the teacher.

The students stand in a circle with their hands behind their back and eyes closed. The teacher places a name tag in each students' hands. On a signal from the teacher, they open their eyes, move around the room, find the student to whom it belongs, and give it to that person. If a student hasn't gotten his name tag, he finds the student who is holding his name tag and retrieves it. Once a student receives his name tag, he places it on his shirt, returns to his original spot in the circle, and sits down.

105. Name Game #1

Although its title lacks imagination, this game, filled with repetition, is an excellent way to ensure the learning of names.

The group stands in a circle. The teacher says, "We're going to a birthday party, and everyone has to bring a gift that begins with the first letter as their name." For example, "My name is Nick, and I'm bringing noisemakers." The person on the right repeats the name and gift of the person before him, and then introduces himself and his gift. "This is Nick, and he's bringing noisemakers. My name is John, and I'm bringing jellybeans." Each person repeats the name of the person and gift that preceded him, and then introduces himself and his gift.

106. Name Game #2

When we associate a gesture with a name, it's easier to remember.

Everyone stands in a circle. One after another, the students say their names and perform a gesture that expresses their personality. If students find it difficult to think of a gesture, they could use a pose or a movement that shows the action involved in a sport, hobby, or activity they enjoy. After everyone has shared their names and gestures, they play a variation of *Tag* using the names and gestures to "tag" someone. One person is "it," perhaps the teacher to start. He tags another person in the circle by saying that person's name and repeating their gesture. That person tags another person and so on. It is important not to repeat anyone's name so all members of the group are included.

107. Name Pantomime

This charade-like game, perfect for the first day of a semester, uses pantomime to assist with learning names.

Students sit in a large circle. Each is given the opportunity to pantomime his name. To begin, one student stands and pantomimes a word for each letter of his name. For example, a student named Dan could pantomime dog for the letter "d," apple for the letter "a," and night for the letter "n." The rest of the students guess each letter and ultimately the student's name.

108. On the Move

Students will be enthralled with the fascinating facts shared by their newfound friends.

Materials: A few rolls of toilet paper

The class is divided into groups of eight or ten, and each group stands in a circle. One person in each group is handed a roll of toilet paper and then tears off one to five pieces, and passes the roll around the circle for everyone to do the same. When everyone in each group has their pieces of toilet paper, they share one interesting fact about themselves for each piece that they're holding. They tear off a piece of toilet paper as they share each interesting fact. For example, if a student has torn off three pieces of toilet paper, he might say, "I know how to juggle. My father is a movie director. I have a pet iguana."

109. People Bingo

This activity is one of the best for meeting new people and learning something about them.

A Bingo grid is created and a copy made for each player. A "free" space appears in the center space. In all the other spaces are descriptive phrases such as "Born in another state" or "Loves to surf." The students move around the room with a pen or pencil to get the signature of a student who meets the criteria for each box in the grid. A person can sign another person's grid in only one box. The first person with a completed grid wins.

Likes broccoli	Has been to Europe	Walks to school	Has read all the Harry Potter books	Has a dog
Is wearing blue	Has eaten sushi	Is left-handed	Wears glasses	Has caught a fish
Speaks a foreign language	Is an only child	**FREE**	Has more than five pets	Was born in another state
Has met a movie star	Plays a musical instrument	Has broken a bone	Loves to surf	Was born in October
Has a swimming pool	Can name the seven dwarfs	Plays a competitive sport	Can ice skate	Has spoken to a grandparent in the last seven days

110. Singing Name Game

This game will provide unforgettable moments and ensure the learning of names.

Players get into a big circle. The teacher tells them, "On the count of three, sing out your first name as loudly as you can. Ready? One, two, three!" The students and teacher sing at the same time.

Next, the players create a short movement sequence that can be done in the same amount of time that it takes to sing out their name. It can be one continuous movement or a quick series of smaller movements. The teacher demonstrates. The players are given a few minutes to leave the circle and create a movement and rehearse it. Everyone comes back into the circle and shares their name and movement one at a time.

It's important for the names to be shared quickly, and it's fine if someone starts before another player is finished. The fast pace prevents the activity from becoming a performance of various routines and keeps it lively.

111. That's Me

What a fun, simple game to play during the first week of class, or anytime!

Preparation: A list of people's traits, characteristics, likes, and dislikes is created. See *People Bingo*.

Students sit in their usual classroom arrangement. The teacher calls out something from the list. Anyone to whom the statements apply stands up.

Statements
I'm the oldest child in my family.
I walk to school.
I have a dog.
I have a cat.
I like pizza.
I have read at least one Harry Potter book.
I wear glasses.
I like to surf.

Chapter Eight

Observation

"A lot of acting is paying attention ... "
— *Robert Redford*

Upon being quizzed about our campus, most of my middle school students didn't know the color of the trash cans they walked by several times a day, or the title of the bulletin board on the wall inside the theatre classroom door. Most of us don't notice our surroundings as we go about our daily activities. It's possible to improve one's powers of observation, but it takes determination to be focused on the moment at hand to take in the details of one's surroundings.

For an actor to create believable characters, he must be an acute observer of his surroundings, using all five senses. His studied observations will serve him well as he takes on the challenge of creating realistic characters. To play an old man, for example, an actor does his best to recall how an old person moves, sits, and talks.

Opportunities abound during the course of daily living to not only recall visual details, particularly about people, but also to recall details related to the other four senses: smell, taste, touch, and hearing. To become a more adept observer, an actor can participate in many varied activities and make an effort to discover new things around him. The following warm-ups can aid an actor in becoming more alert and observant.

112. Ball Toss

Success in this observation game will depend on following directions and using eye contact.

Materials: Five to ten small, soft balls in a transportable container

Students stand in a circle. The teacher makes eye contact with a player across the circle and throws him a ball. The ball makes its way back and forth across the circle with players making eye contact with someone across the circle before throwing the ball. Periodically throughout the game, the teacher introduces one additional ball at a time until there are five or six moving back and forth across the circle at the same time. Encourage the students to concentrate on throwing the ball accurately and then to scan the circle continuously to allow someone with a ball to be able to communicate with them through eye contact. This warm-up is most successful when played with little or no talking.

113. Concentration Circle

Actors must be alert and observant, and playing this warm-up will help to strengthen observation skills.

Students form a large circle and number sequentially starting with one. Because they are going to shout numbers across the circle within an established rhythm, they agree on a gesture that will facilitate the number exchange. For example, right hand up, right hand down.

The player who is chosen to begin raises his right hand while shouting a number such as twenty-two and then puts his hand down. The player with that number raises his right hand while shouting another number, such as eight, and so on. The same number can be repeated, but the game continues until every player's number has been called. Players who don't respond when their number is called sit in the middle of the circle. The teacher begins the game again or chooses someone else to call a number. What often happens is that players call the number of someone who is out. Doing so causes them to be out also, so being observant is very important.

114. Garden of Statues

Students will enjoy this classic observation game.

Players spread out in a large space. One person is the pointer and all other players form a Garden of Statues by striking a pose. They then try to move from one pose to another without getting caught by the pointer. They cannot speak or make sounds of any kind. If the pointer sees them moving or hears them making sounds, they are out. The pointer moves around the Garden of Statues trying to get the players to laugh or smile or otherwise break character. He may not touch them, but he can talk, tell jokes, mimic them, or use whatever appropriate strategy he can to get them to move. He does his best to be quick, turning around at random to try to catch the statues changing poses. When the pointer sees statues move, they are out, and quietly step outside the playing area. The last statue remaining is the winner and becomes the pointer if there is time to play another round.

115. Group Stop

A type of freeze game, this warm-up gets students moving and requires that they be observant.

Everyone quietly moves around the room. After milling around for about twenty seconds, anyone in the group can elect to freeze unexpectedly. As soon as the other players notice that someone else has frozen, they freeze as well. Once everyone is frozen, the group is given a cue to start moving around again. They must keep moving about for twenty seconds before someone else freezes. The goal is to see how quickly the group can freeze in position after someone stops.

116. Make It Real

This exercise is useful to give young actors an opportunity to practice using sensory recall, which they call upon in the creation of believable situations.

Everyone sits in a large circle on chairs or on the floor. The teacher names an imaginary object for all the students to hold. As they hold the imaginary object, questions like the following are asked, and the students concentrate on answering the questions silently, using their imagination:

How heavy is it?
What color is it?
How does it feel? Scratchy? Soft? Smooth?
What is its temperature?
How does it smell?

Does it have any taste?
Can you hear it?
Can you make any sound by tapping on it?

After the students have concentrated on answering the questions silently, the teacher may ask several players to share their answers. To continue the warm-up, the teacher names another imaginary object for the students to hold, and the questioning process begins again.

Imaginary Objects

Ice cream cone, kitten, sharp knife, cup of hot chocolate, ice cold glass of lemonade, slice of pizza, pail of water, stuffed toy panda, new tennis ball, round balloon, warm washcloth, hand puppet, flashlight, candy bar, seashell, yo-yo, water gun, beach ball, cell phone, baby bird, paint brush, five-pound dumbbell, feather, newspaper, hairbrush, brick, rose, bar of soap, CD, S.O.S. pad.

117. Observation Memory

This warm-up is not difficult but stimulates quick thinking and alertness.

Players and the teacher stand in a large circle. The first player starts by calling out the name of an animal. Then the next player calls out the name of a different animal beginning with the last letter of the animal previously named. For example, Player 1 says "cat," Player 2 says "tiger," Player 3 says "rat," and so on around the circle. No animal can be named twice. This game can be played using other categories like items of clothing, towns, flowers, rock stars, breeds of dog, and names.

118. Pass a Gesture

When students pass a gesture, emphasis is on accurate observation and imitation.

Students and teacher stand in a circle. The teacher initiates a gesture, any movement at all. The person to the right imitates the movement without changing it in any way. He then passes it to the student on his right, and the gesture in turn continues to be passed around the circle. Each student imitates the original movement until it comes back to the teacher. The students' goal is to duplicate exactly what they see, not adding any of their own personalities or expressions. If the gesture is changed in any way, the teacher stops the warm-up and starts over.

119. Red Ball

An exercise in pantomime provides an excellent challenge to students' observation skills. This game is a great warm-up during a unit on pantomime.

Basic Red Ball

Players stand in a big circle. The teacher pantomimes pulling a small ball, about the size of a tennis ball, out of his pocket. It's important that he portrays the weight, size, and texture of the ball accurately. He then pretends to toss it to another player, remembering to use eye contact first, and says "red ball." The player receiving it acknowledges the transfer by saying "red ball" and tosses it to another player, and so on.

Intermediate Red Ball

The teacher introduces two or three other balls of different colors to the circle one at a time by saying the new color as he tosses it. As the imaginary balls are tossed around the circle, it is a challenge for students to keep track of what color they have.

Advanced Red Ball

After the imaginary balls have been tossed for a while, other imaginary objects of different sizes and shapes are introduced to the circle. As the objects are tossed, it is important for students to keep track of what object they have received.

120. Ring on a String

This is another classic observation party game adapted for the classroom.

Materials: A long piece of string, a ring without gems or stones

Preparation: The teacher needs to create a giant circular loop with string so that the ring can slide freely. The loop needs to be big enough for all the students to hold on to it with both hands.

Players stand in a circle. Each player in the circle holds the string in both hands and practices making a left to right sliding motion, touching the fists of the person on either side of him while passing the ring from person to person; the string doesn't move. Someone is then chosen to stand in the middle of the circle, and that student closes his eyes for a few seconds so students can take some time to move the ring around the circle. Each player continuously makes the motions of passing the ring along the string, whether or not they are holding the ring. Then the person in the center watches the other players as they are "moving" the ring. When he says "freeze," the players must stop moving the ring and he has three guesses to determine who has the ring. If he is right, the person who was holding the ring takes his place in the center. If he doesn't find the ring, it is passed along the string again, and then he has three more chances to guess.

121. Sensory Overload

This game tests students' observation skills, but also takes all of one's senses to the limit. The purpose is to keep the actions moving around the circle while maintaining a consistent rhythmical cadence.

Materials: A small, soft ball and several objects like scissors, a vase, or a candle

Players stand in a circle. A ball is passed from person to person around the circle in a consistent pattern and rhythm. It is important that no matter what happens, the ball is continuously passed without interruption around the circle. The ball is passed once or twice around the circle so students can feel the rhythmical cadence that needs to be maintained as other actions are introduced.

After the rhythm is established, the teacher introduces a simple gesture, like doffing a hat, and passes an object in addition to the ball around the circle to the right. He then introduces another simple gesture, like shaking his fist, and passes a different object around the circle in the opposite direction, to the left. When a player receives an object, he imitates the action and passes the object to the next player.

As many actions and objects as possible are passed around the circle in both directions to create "sensory overload." As objects make their way back to the leader, they can be removed one by one until the ball is the only remaining item going around the circle.

122. Squeezer

The person in the center of the circle has the opportunity to test his observation skills.

Everyone gets into a circle and holds hands. One player stands in the center. The game begins with one player gently squeezing the hand of his neighbor to the left when the person in the center is not looking. The receiver of the squeeze then squeezes the hand of his neighbor to the left, thus creating a "squeeze wave" around the circle. If the player in the middle spots a person who is passing a squeeze, the squeezer exchanges places with him in the center of the circle.

123. This Is a Scissors

There are many versions of this game. The following is a version that works well and encourages players to concentrate and observe details closely.

Materials: A pair of scissors

Players and teacher sit on chairs in a circle. The teacher holds a pair of scissors and explains that the scissors will be passed open or closed from one player to another around the circle. He tells the students that in this game they must observe him very closely so they can be successful in passing the scissors. Then he crosses his ankles, passes the closed scissors to the student on the right, and says, "Passing closed." The next player passes the scissors either open or closed to the next person in the circle. If he passes the scissors closed, he says, "Passing closed" and he should have his ankles crossed. If he passes the scissors open and says, "Passing open" he should have his ankles uncrossed.

After each player passes the scissors, the teacher and those students who have played the game before tell the player whether or not he has correctly passed the scissors. Players will want to repeat this game again, and on another day it might be fun to pass another object in a different way and/or let a student start the game. The next time students play this game they will be keenly observant.

124. Up, Jenkins

I have no idea why this game is called Up, Jenkins. *It is similar to* Ring on a String, *except that it is played with a small object rather than a length of string and a ring.*

Materials: A small object that can be passed around the circle

Students sit in a big circle on the floor. One player stands in the middle of the circle. The players in the circle sit with their hands behind their backs, and one of them holds a small object. They pass the object from hand to hand behind their backs. The player in the middle moves around the circle watching the players carefully in order to detect the person who has the object. The players in the circle can pretend to pass an object and distract the player in the middle. If the player in the middle thinks he knows where the object is, he must tap that person's hand. If the guess is correct, he exchanges places with the person caught with the object. If the guess is wrong, he must remain in the center of the circle and the game continues.

125. Who Started the Motion?

This is another of many excellent observation games.

One player leaves the room. The others sit or stand in a circle. Someone initiates a rhythmical movement using hands, arms, head, body, or legs that the students copy. The movement is changed periodically and kept slow and deliberate. The students are encouraged not to look directly at the leader but to use peripheral vision to keep track of changes in movement. The player who has left the room returns and stands in the center of the circle. His task is to observe the other players very closely so he can determine who is leading the movements. It is the task of the whole group to stay together without giving away who the leader is. When the person in the center correctly guesses the leader, they exchange places, and the game continues as it began except instead of leaving the room, the new person in the center can close his eyes and the group can silently designate someone else to lead the motions.

Tips for the Lead Person

Make gradual changes instead of abrupt ones.
Maintain a neutral expression.
Introduce new, creative movements.

126. Yes!

Need a game that encourages observation, concentration, and cooperation? This is it!

Everyone stands still in a circle facing towards the center. When the group is quiet and focused, the teacher demonstrates making a sound and movement. For example, he takes a small step while lifting both hands and pushing forward with fingers tipped up and palms facing the center. As his hands reach the point where they are completely outstretched, he gives a little extra push, creating a short, sharp action, and shouts, "Yes!" Everyone practices the movement and sound several times with the teacher. The purpose of the game is for everyone to anticipate when the movement is going to happen so that they imitate the action and make the sound at the same time. The group will be so focused on the teacher that they'll be able to sense when he is going to move. The challenge is for everyone to be in sync. Students also will enjoy leading this warm-up.

Chapter Nine
Pantomime

"It's good to shut up sometimes."
— Marcel Marceau

Dennis Caltagirone defined pantomime in his book *Theatre Arts: The Dynamics of Acting* as "a sequence of facial expressions, gestures, body positions and movements that convey a story or character without words." It sounds so simple, but those who have tried to pantomime making a peanut butter and jelly sandwich know it's not so easy. There is a tendency to take for granted the many minute details that go into a seemingly mundane task. Doing pantomime well is an art! Not only does pantomime take astute observation, but it also requires a strong memory of physical and sensory details and the ability to duplicate those details without objects.

It is thought that prehistoric man is likely the first to have used pantomime because of rudimentary verbal skills that made physical gestures and facial expressions paramount to getting his message across. During the Golden Age of Greece, theatres became so large that spoken words couldn't always be heard, therefore skillful pantomime by Greek actors was necessary to convey meaning to vast audiences. In the Middle Ages, small pantomime groups wandered from place to place performing wherever they could find an audience. Also during this period the court jester was adept at pantomime.

It was during the Renaissance that pantomime thrived. Travelling actors used bare plot outlines and performed them using an artful combination of improv and pantomime. Commedia dell'Arte, known as improvised comedy, was filled with stock characters like Pierrot, Harlequin, and Pantalone who created clever speeches combined with a masterfully performed pantomime routine.

Silent film greats like Charlie Chaplin, Laurel and Hardy, Buster Keaton, Harold Lloyd, and the Marx Brothers inspired Marcel Marceau with their mesmerizing and entertaining use of pantomime. Marceau, who was referred to as the world's greatest mime said, "A good mime should be able to make the audience feel that the imaginary world that he is creating is real."

The following games have been adapted for easy use as group warm-ups for the study of pantomime.

127. Anything Fabric

This is a simple but creative warm-up to do early in a unit on pantomime.

Materials: A bandana or small square piece of fabric

Students stand in a circle and the teacher holds up a piece of fabric and says, "What could this piece of fabric be? We're going to pass it around the circle and each of you gets to show us something that it could become. You may transform it into anything and pantomime how to use it." For example, the teacher could demonstrate pantomiming a matador using the fabric and say, "This is a bullfighting cape." The fabric is then passed from person to person, with each one pantomiming a use for the piece of fabric and stating what it is. No one may repeat what someone else has said; every idea needs to be unique.

Ideas
A Superman cape
A diaper
A turban
A rug
An apron

Variation: Limit ideas to clothing or things that are the color of the fabric.

128. First Day Group Pantomime

Although originally a performance exercise, this works well as a warm-up because it gives students time to move around, work in groups, and engage in lighthearted pantomime.

Materials: Index cards, basket

Preparation: The teacher writes a general group activity on the index cards and puts them in the basket.

The students organize themselves into groups of four or five. After the students have created groups, one student from each group picks an index card from the basket. The students' goal is to communicate the general activity by having each actor in the group pantomime a related specific activity. For example, five actors could perform the general activity of "basic training" by pantomiming doing jumping jacks, climbing a rope, saluting, crawling under a fence, and polishing boots. The groups are given five to ten minutes to brainstorm and rehearse. Each group performs their pantomime for the rest of the students. After each performance, the audience guesses the general activity and the specific activity that each member of the group performed.

General Activities
Housework
Building a house
Gardening
At the beach
Camping
Circus acts
Office work
Performing with a band

129. The Martha Game

No one seems to know who Martha is or how this game got its name, but it's a major hit with students and can be played anytime or during a unit on pantomime.

If a class is larger than twenty-five, the students are divided into two teams so one team can perform for the other. Students sit facing the stage or acting area. The students are told that they are going to form a human painting. One person runs into the playing space, positions himself, announces what he is in the painting, and freezes in that position. For example, he might run in and say, "I'm a tree," and then freeze. Immediately after, another person runs into the space and forms something else that could be found in the same painting, such as, "I'm a bench," and freezes. The remaining students add to the painting until every member of the group is part of the picture. When all the students in the first group have moved into the acting space, their creation is enthusiastically applauded. Then the second group creates a new masterpiece.

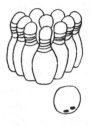

130. Mime It Down the Alley

The players try to communicate an object to each other so that the last person in line has the same "message" as the first.

Materials: Index cards cut in half

Preparation: An object is written on each index card.

Players are divided into groups of six to eight people and arranged in a single file seated on the floor. No one is allowed to talk at any point in the game. The first person in each line is given an index card with an object written on it. The other players are instructed to turn around to face the opposite direction. The first person taps the second person in line on the shoulder. That person turns so the two are facing each other. The first person mimes the object, and when the second person thinks he knows what the object is, he nods. The second person taps the third on the shoulder, they face each other, and the second person mimes the object, and so on down the line. When all the lines are finished, each person at the end of a line is asked to tell the class what he thought the object was. The students also find it interesting to hear what every other person in their line thought the object was. It's important, therefore, for students to continue to remain quiet until the game is completely over. To play again, a different student, perhaps the one at the other end of each line, receives a card and begins to *mime it down the alley*.

Objects
Spaghetti
Clock
Watering can
Bird cage
Envelope
Wig
Toaster
Baby bottle
Balloon
Stapler
Paintbrush
Bug spray

131. Mime Memory

What a delightful way to warm up pantomime skills and to use observation and memory!

Materials: A basket, index cards

Preparation: Simple, everyday tasks or actions written on the index cards.

To begin the warm-up, the group sits in a large circle. The teacher instructs the players to choose a card. Each player moves to a spot in the room to rehearse his pantomime that must be broken down into exactly six movements. The teacher then divides the group into pairs and emphasizes that it is important for players to carefully watch their partners as they mime their task. Then, each member of a pair finds a new partner and performs the mime he observed. After having performed with three or four partners, it is time to observe the results. Volunteers are asked to perform the final mime they observed. The teacher asks if anyone recognizes it as their own, original pantomime. If they do, the player who performed the pantomime does it again and the creator performs his original version. It is interesting for the players to experience the two pantomimes.

Simple Actions
Walking a dog
Sleepwalking
Playing golf
Playing tennis
Painting a room
Washing dishes
Washing a car
Building a campfire
Planting a garden
Setting a table
Wrapping a present
Surfing
Brushing teeth
Pouring a glass of milk

132. Mirror Follow the Leader

This warm-up can be beautiful to watch.

The players stand in a circle. Everyone turns so that they are looking at the back of the next person. One person begins the activity by making simple movements from the waist up. So the movements can be seen, care must be taken to keep his arms to the sides, not in front of him. The player behind the first mirrors the movements, but with a delay of about a second. The third person mirrors the second, again with a one second delay, and so on around the circle. Eventually, the person who began will see his own movements recreated by the person in front of him, but delayed by a time interval. The effect is like a wave of movement making its way around the circle. For the player who initiates the movement, the reward is seeing that movement come back to him. The teacher does not participate but plays the role of observer in order to be sure the wave is making its way around the circle. A few players could be pulled out of the group so they can watch from inside the circle.

133. Mirror Game

This game is consistently successful and popular. After doing this warm-up, students may enjoy watching the classic episode of I Love Lucy *called "Lucy and Harpo" in which the two actors play a humorous version of the* Mirror Game.

The class is divided into pairs, A and B, facing each other. The game works better if partners are close to the same height. B is a person looking in a mirror, and A is that person's image in the mirror. A reflects all movements initiated by B, including facial expressions. Movements are slow and expansive. B is not out to trick A; the goal is for the partners to work together. The objective is for their movements to be so well timed and fluid that an observer would not be able to tell which person is initiating the actions. Playing a slow piece of classical music is helpful to inspire slow actions and help to keep students focused. After one to two minutes, A and B switch roles.

134. Movement Telephone

This warm-up, a movement version of the telephone game, is a simpler version of Mime It Down the Alley, *and just as much fun.*

The class is divided into groups of ten players. Each group stands in single file, facing the front of the room. The teacher stands at the back of the lines, and asks the last person in each line to turn and face him. The teacher performs a very simple series of hand movements. The last player in each line taps the next person in line, who turns around and the movement is passed on. Eventually, in this manner, the movement makes its way to the front of the lines. The teacher asks each of the players who are at the front of the line to demonstrate the movement to the rest of the groups. He then shows the players what the original movement looked like. The person in each line who first performed the pantomime moves to the front of the line and the game can be played again.

135. The Movement Experiment

This warm-up focuses on the fact that a movement can be changed in many specific ways.

Optional Materials: CD player, music of various speeds

Students pick a spot to stand somewhere in the room and practice the following changes in the way they walk, which are cued by the teacher:
- Simply walk throughout the room as they naturally walk, making sure to focus on their own walk, staying about five feet away from anyone else.
- Change the *size* of their movement. They can make the walk wider or narrower by widening or narrowing their stance and swinging their arms farther away or closer to their body. They can make their walk higher or lower by walking on tiptoe or slouching. They can make their walk deeper by taking larger steps or swinging their arms farther forward or back.

- Change the *timing*. They make their walk faster or slower.
- Change the *weight*. An angry person may walk heavily; a ballerina may move lightly.
- Change *direction*. Their walk can be direct, moving to a specific point without veering off the path, or indirect, wandering aimlessly.
- Change the *tension*. As they walk, their muscles can be loose and relaxed or tense and constricted.
- Change the *shape* or the kind of *movement*. This involves actually changing to a different movement. For example, a walk could become a run or a crawl; arms could stop swinging or relaxed hands could be changed into fists.

Variation: This warm-up could lead into a game in which the teacher creates a short movement sequence. For example, he could walk four steps, bend, and tie his shoe. The whole group practices this sequence. Next, someone volunteers to change it by making only one change and everyone practices the new sequence. Other students volunteer to make a change and the group practices the sequence after each. The movement sequence will become less and less like the original and will evolve into something else.

136. Object

This is a fun, fast paced game great for practicing miming skills and stimulating the imagination.

Materials: Interesting objects such as a rolling pin, whisk, Frisbee, or a funnel

Players sit in a large circle. The teacher places an object, like a rolling pin, in the center of the circle. The purpose of the game is to act out a five second scene in which the object is transformed into something other than what it is. Players can either take turns or jump in to do a scene with the object. For example, if the object is a shoe, an actor could use it as a telephone, or someone else might use it as a paint brush. The game continues until all players have participated.

Variation: Several objects at the same time could be introduced into play.

137. Open the Door

Door opening can be a fascinating subject for pantomime.

The class is divided into groups of ten to twelve players. One group lines up across the stage, from right to left, and the rest of the students play the role of observer. The teacher asks the players to think of a way to open a door, having a specific door in mind so they can make the pantomime realistic. One at a time, the players mime opening the door. The teacher challenges them to do it in a way that is distinctly different from any of the others. The rest of the students may be invited to make observations about the opening of the imaginary doors. Could they tell what kind of door was being opened? How? Did the emotional state of the person opening the door provide a clue? Mimes and observers are rotated until everyone has had a chance to open a door.

138. Rhyme Charades

Although it sounds simple, this warm-up challenges young minds.

Students sit in a circle. The teacher starts by saying, "I am thinking of a word that rhymes with (insert word)." For example, he can say, "I am thinking of a word that rhymes with cat." Anyone who thinks he knows the word that the teacher could be thinking of raises his hand. When called upon, he does not say the word, but goes into the center of the circle and pantomimes his guess. For example, he could pantomime a bat by flapping his arms and swooping. The students in the circle take turns guessing what word the student in the center is pantomiming. If the word is guessed, but it's not the one the teacher is thinking of, another student is called on to pantomime. When a student correctly pantomimes the word the teacher is thinking of and the students correctly guess it, the round is over and the teacher picks a new word. The warm-up continues with the teacher offering new words. Two rhyme words that work well for this game are *oat* and *air*.

139. Sound Circle

This game works well in a unit on pantomime or voice, or it's just fun to play anytime.

Everyone gets into a big circle. One player starts the game by making a gesture and a sound that the person on his right immediately mimics. After the second player mimics the first, he then turns to his neighbor on the right and creates a totally different gesture and sound. Players mimic only the gesture and sound of the person to their right. Gestures and sounds continue in that manner around the circle. This game is livelier if players turn to their neighbor and pass a new gesture and sound as fast as possible without imitating the gesture and sound they received.

140. Statues

Emphasis in this warm-up is on slow, deliberate movement with attention to detail.

Students stand in a circle with their hands at their sides and feet about shoulder width apart. The teacher leads the warm-up by naming an emotional state, such as nervousness, anger, or pride. Students then have ten seconds to slowly move into a posture that expresses the emotional state in as much detail as possible. After the teacher counts to ten, they freeze. Another emotion is chosen and the students repeat the warm-up.

141. Ten-Second Objects

Creating large inanimate objects presents a delightful challenge for student mimes.

The students are divided into groups of four or five and spread themselves throughout the room. The teacher calls out the name of an object and each group makes the shape of that object using their bodies, while he counts down slowly from ten to zero. After ten seconds the groups must be completely frozen in position.

Objects

A car
A ship
A blender
A washing machine
A clock

Variation: Groups create an object that uses movement.

142. All Together

To become an inanimate object is an excellent and fun challenge for a young actor.

Everyone sits in a large space on the floor or on a stage. The teacher explains that the group will pantomime together a group action and may have the creative opportunity to become an inanimate object. For example, the teacher could say, "Everyone is ice cream melting." The students stand quietly in the large space and become melting ice cream. Next, the teacher or a volunteer calls out another group action. Some ideas are: popcorn popping, balloons deflating, marbles rolling, eggs hatching, or fireworks going off. If the group is large, it can be divided in half and the audience can try to guess what the performers are doing.

143. Walk My Walk

In this warm-up young actors have fun with stereotypical character walks.

Materials: Index cards, a basket

Preparation: Types of people with unique walks written on the index cards and put in the basket.

Players stand in a big circle. The group discusses the many ways different types of people walk. For example, a clown walks with exaggerated movements and large steps because his shoes are big and a cowboy walks bowlegged because he's ridden a horse for many years. Each player draws a card from the basket. As each player walks across the circle several times performing the walk of the person on his card, the group tries to guess his identity. When someone guesses correctly, the entire group imitates the walk, and then forms into a circle again to watch another player do a different walk.

Walks

Tightrope walker
Old person
Fashion model
Infant learning to walk
Burglar

144. Walking Through

This warm-up provides unusual situations for walking.

Students spread themselves throughout the room. The teacher calls out any or all of the following situations, and the students use their imagination to create interesting walks:

Through a dark, dangerous alley
Through a huge bowl of whipping cream
Across a room of bouncy springs
Through tall underbrush
Underwater
In the desert, looking for water
Through a bowl of chewed-up bubble gum
Barefoot on fine, hot sand
With your right foot stuck in a bucket
Across a street of broken glass
Through a forest of man-eating plants
Through a snowstorm

145. Weather Walks

What a wonderful opportunity to pantomime movement using multiple sensory recall.

Everyone moves around the space, quietly walking at a brisk pace. The warm-up begins with students engaging in their normal style of walking. Then, as the teacher calls out a weather pattern, everyone changes his walk to suit the type of weather.

Types of Weather
A hot, sticky summer heat
A cool, spring breeze
A cold winter wind during a snowstorm
A perfect summer day
A rainstorm
A hurricane

In addition to weather conditions, students can also walk in the following environments:
A steep, rocky mountain top
Underwater
A dark forest at night
The Amazon jungle
New York City
The moon
A frozen lake

146. What Are You Doing?

Because the instructions for this classic pantomime warm-up are longer than most, it may appear complicated, but it is not difficult to play and will be one of the most memorable for students.

Level One
The group forms a circle. To begin, a player pantomimes a simple activity, for example, brushing his teeth. The person on his right asks him, "What are you doing?" The first student replies with anything *except* what he is actually doing. For example, he might say, "I'm

washing my pet elephant." As soon as the player on his right hears the answer, he must begin to pantomime the mentioned activity, in this case it's washing an elephant. The person next to him asks, "What are you doing?" and so on around the circle.

Some pointers:
The person acting must not stop until he has answered the question.
The new person must start immediately when the answer is heard.
The answer must not be what the person is doing or something that looks like what he is actually doing.

Level Two
Play in the same way as Level One with one addition. The original formula is "I'm _____." Add to it, "I'm _____ with a _____." For example, "I'm washing my pet elephant with a broom."

Level Three
Play in the same way as Level One and Two, but add one more detail. When asked, "What are you doing?" the students reply, "I'm _____ with a _____ while _____." For example, "I'm washing my pet elephant with a broom while playing tennis."

147. What's My Job?

In this warm-up with a twist, young actors pantomime professions.

Materials: Index cards, a basket

Preparation: Choose fifteen professions, write each profession on two index cards — a total of thirty index cards — and place them in a basket. Adjust the number of cards according to the number of students in the group.

Students sit in a circle. Each student takes a card out of the basket, making sure not to show anyone. On a cue from the teacher, all of the players move into the acting space and mime their occupation. Their task is to spot the person with the same occupation as theirs. When they spot the person, they approach him, and without speaking, check that they are both miming the same job. If they are, they sit down together. The game continues until everybody is sitting down. To conclude the warm-up, the teacher checks to make sure that partners mimed the same profession by asking them to tell each other and the rest of the students their profession.

148. Yes, Let's

Often students will want to play this warm-up more than once.

The class spreads throughout the classroom or acting area. Someone picks a group activity, like going to a birthday party. Related to the activity, one player might say, "Let's play Pin the Tail on the Donkey." Everyone chimes in, "Yes, let's," and all the players pantomime playing *Pin the Tail on the Donkey*. A second player could jump in and suggest another activity like, "Let's blow out the candles." All the players say, "Yes, let's" and pantomime blowing out candles. A third player jumps in and suggests another activity that could be done at a birthday party and so on. When they run out of ideas, the students come up with another group activity, and the game continues.

Chapter Ten
Stretching and Relaxation

"For fast-acting relief, try slowing down."
— Lily Tomlin

In my middle school theatre class on the day of a rehearsal or performance, students often enter the room in a flurry, talking loudly, with arms and legs akimbo. "I am so not ready," insists Mary as she flops into her chair. "I don't know my lines," laments Ellen. "I am so freaked," exclaims Alex. An appearance on-stage in front of an expectant audience can feel threatening, especially to a beginning actor, and it is not unusual for an actor to experience stage fright no matter how small the performance.

One way to harness nervous energy and use it creatively is by learning and practicing relaxation techniques. Famous acting teacher, Lee Strasberg, believed that tension is the actor's greatest enemy; therefore, relaxation exercises should be done before every rehearsal and every show.

There are many ways to become more relaxed. One of the best is to perform simple stretches accompanied by calming breathing techniques like the ones presented in this section. Stretching accompanied by controlled breathing will help reduce muscle tension and improve coordination by allowing for freer and easier movement, help develop necessary body awareness, and aid in feeling ready for action.

It is on rehearsal days or the days of a performance that stretching and relaxation warm-ups help alleviate nervousness so that "butterflies are flying in formation."

149. Balloon Blow-Up

In addition to being a good all around body warm-up, Balloon Blow-Up can be used to the students' delight during a unit or lesson on pantomime.

Students spread out in the playing space, making sure they are about an arm's length away from anyone else. The teacher asks them to concentrate on the color, shape, and feel of a new balloon. The teacher says, "You are to become that balloon, starting from an empty state. I'll pretend to be the person blowing up the balloon. Now lie down on the floor." The teacher begins blowing, and the students pantomime being balloons slowly filling with air. When they look like they are reaching full capacity, the teacher says, "You should be completely filled up with air on the last of three blows that I make." The teacher blows three more times and says, "Freeze!" Then the teacher yells "puncture," and the students move around the room like deflating balloons, being sure not to interfere with the movement of the other balloons, and come to rest lying on the floor.

150. Big Numbers

Students will experience a wonderful stretching workout by doing this warm-up.

Players spread throughout the room or stand in a big circle. They pretend to hold a large piece of chalk in their right hand and write the numbers one through nine in the air as large as possible. As the teacher calls out each number, the players write them slowly, bending, stretching, and reaching so that they're using their whole body. They repeat, using the left hand. It's also fun and an even better stretch to write numbers with elbows, head, fingers, arms, hips, and the whole body.

151. Body Spelling

Before participating in performance activities, students enjoy this fun way of limbering up.

Students stand in a spot somewhere in the classroom or playing area. The teacher instructs them to slowly spell their first and last name using their entire body. They are encouraged to form each letter with lots of stretching, bending, and reaching.

152. The Cord Through the Body

This clever movement works well to involve students in a simple, effective relaxing stretch at the beginning of a class or after intense brainstorming, rehearsal, or performance.

Students stand to face the teacher who delivers the following script and the students do their best to move accordingly:

Pretend there is a cord running through the center of your body that comes out the top of your head. With this cord through you, feel how it keeps you in balance. Move your body, swaying back and forth, bouncing up and down on the cord. Think of yourself as a puppet with someone above you pulling on the cord, moving your body, head, arms, and feet. Feel a wind come along and blow you. Then feel the rain and hail falling on you. Finally, the sun is warming you.

After this exercise students will be limber and ready for action.

153. Let Go!

Tightening and relaxing muscles can aid in alleviating restlessness or nervousness.

Everyone sits facing the teacher who talks the group through the following:

- Tighten your right fist. Feel the tension. Now release your fist and let your hand go limp. Feel the relaxation. Repeat with your left hand.
- Bend your right arm and tighten your fist and biceps. Hold it tight and feel the tension in your arm. Release the tension and let your arm hang loose. Feel the relaxation. Now repeat with your left arm.
- Close your eyes tightly. Really scrunch them closed. Now open your eyes and relax the tension. Clench your teeth. Feel the pressure in your jaw. Now release your jaw and feel the relaxation.
- Pull your shoulders up to your ears and tense the entire shoulder and neck area really tightly. Relax. Breathe out. Repeat.
- Inhale deeply. Don't let your shoulders move. Keep your hand on your belly and feel it expand so you know you're using your diaphragm. Hold the breath tight in your lungs. Release and feel the flow of relaxation. Repeat two more times. Exhale. Relax.
- Tighten your stomach muscles; hold the tension. Release and relax. Again, tighten the stomach muscles and relax.

• Straighten your legs, tighten your thighs, and point your toes hard. Hold. Release the tension, and let your feet gently rest on the floor. Feel the relaxation. Straighten your legs, tighten your thighs, and pull up your toes and really stretch. Feel the tension in your whole leg. Release the tension, and let your feet gently rest on the floor. Feel the relaxation.

• Now, as best you can while sitting, relax your body completely, allowing it to go limp. Let your hands rest in your lap. Let your head gently fall to your chest. Do a body scan from the top of your head to your toes to make sure all your muscles are relaxed. Take three slow, deep breaths.

Good job!

154. Movin' and Groovin'

An actor strives for a relaxed body and voice so this warm-up would be ideal before students perform.

Students stand in a spot in the room where they are at least an arm's length apart from anyone else and are facing the teacher, who conducts this short relaxing warm-up:

Rag Doll: With feet apart in a comfortable balance, stretch up tall. Now bend over by collapsing quickly and loosely from the waist with your relaxed arms and hands dangling to the floor. Keep your arms, hands, and neck completely relaxed like a rag doll. Slowly raise up, staying relaxed. Repeat two or three times.

Head Roll: With your chin close to your chest, slowly rotate your head to the left, back, right, and down in front again. Reverse the rotation. Be sure to keep your neck relaxed, letting your head roll like a dead weight in a socket.

Arm Swing: Begin with arms relaxed at your sides. First, slowly swing your right arm forward and around five times. Repeat with your left arm. Now let's do the same thing, only backwards. Be gentle and make sure your movements are slow. Swing your right arm up and back around five times. Do the same with your left arm. Lastly, slowly swing both arms backwards five times. Shake out your arms.

Yawn: Slowly yawn, quietly saying "ahhhh." The sound you make is a relaxed sound.

155. Pinocchio

The following warm-up is a delightful narrative pantomime of Pinocchio slowly coming to life. It's unique in that it's a physical warm-up and stretching exercise with dramatic content to keep it focused.

The students stand quietly facing the front of the room where the teacher conducts the warm-up by saying the following:

- Right now you're made completely of wood. Your arms and legs are carved from a single piece of wood. You can't move any part of your body.
- Now the magic has begun. It begins at the top of your head. The spell moves down slowly until the tip of your head to your eyebrows is flesh and blood. Move your eyebrows.
- The spell keeps moving down. Now you can move your eyes. All your life you've been staring straight ahead, and now you can look to the sides.
- The spell gets to your ears and your nose. Wiggle them.
- The spell gets to your mouth. You can smile. It feels strange at first, and probably looks pretty strange too, but you grow more comfortable with it. Try some other facial expressions as well, like a frown, look of surprise, or confusion.
- Slowly, you discover that you can turn your head. Careful! You can look up and down carefully as well. Look! You have feet.
- The spell reaches your shoulders. But remember, your arms and hands are still attached to your torso since you are carved from a single piece of wood, so you can move *only* your shoulders. Try some circles. Do you feel a tingle up and down your spine? That's the magic working.
- The spell reaches your chest. You can puff it out like a soldier.
- Your elbows can move now, but still not your hands. As the spell goes lower, see if you can pull your left hand away from your body. Good! You did it.
- Bring your hand up to your face and study it. See if you can move the fingers. Wow, you've never seen anything so beautiful! See if you can get your right hand free as well. Does it move too?
- The spell has reached your waist. Carefully bend forward and to the side. See if you can bend backwards and if you can make a circle.
- The spell reaches your hips. Move them around and around and back and forth, but remember, your knees are still locked together and your feet are still attached to your pedestal.

- The spell gets to your knees. See if they bend. Reach down and see if you can pull your left foot free. Now point your toe. Flex your foot. Make little circles. Now see if you can get your right foot free. Flex it and make little circles.
- You're all real now! See how you can move. Careful at first; these are your first steps. Let's find all the ways your new body moves.

156. Shakety Shake

Tension builds up during a day at school. This is a fun way to loosen up.

Everyone stands and faces the teacher who delivers and leads the following:

- Begin by shaking your feet, right foot first and then your left foot. Next, shake the entire leg, right and then left. Really concentrate on letting each leg relax and shake floppily.
- Next, shake your right hand and forearm, slowly and gently at first and then vigorously. Then let your right arm dangle at your side and shake it gently and then more vigorously and then gently again. Do the same with your left arm.
- The next part of Shakety Shake feels really good. Don't be shy during this part. Shake your hips from left to right just like you're doing *The Twist* that was popular in the '60s. First, try to isolate just the hips. Then add your waist and torso and your chest. Don't let your arms dangle at your sides. Bend them at the elbow and let them get involved too.
- Do vigorous shoulder shrugs. Then gently shake your head, slowly at first and then faster. Be careful not to shake with too much of a jerking motion.
- Now for the best part: Shake your entire body from feet to head. Stop shaking and relax. Close your eyes. Take three slow deep breaths. Hold your hand on your belly to make sure you're not using your shoulders. Inhale — tummy moves out — and exhale — tummy moves in. Inhale. Exhale. Inhale. Exhale.

You're all shook up!

157. The Tingler

This tension releasing warm-up is similar to Shakety Shake, *but shorter.*

Everyone stands facing the teacher who gives the following instructions:
- Shake your hands hard from the wrists down. Not the whole arm, just the wrist. Shake. Shake. Hard. Harder. Even harder. Are they tingling?
- Stop shaking and reach for the ceiling and stretch up with both arms. Up, up, up. Pull. Pull. Up on your toes. Make a straight line from the tip of your fingers to your toes. If you feel yourself wobbling, just pull up to steady yourself. Higher, higher. Another quarter of an inch. Hold. Are you tingling?
- Now slowly move down. *Sloooowly* down. Come slowly down on your heels and bring your arms down to your sides. Relax and sit down.

158. Walking Around the Space

This warm-up is a good way to encourage focus and to simply get players on their feet and moving.

Without talking, the players walk around the space and are encouraged to notice as much as possible about the room. As they pass each other, students may look at each other and smile, but they must keep moving.

Walking Variations
Walk sideways.
Walk backwards.
Walk in straight lines and only change direction at a right angle.
Walk as meandering as possible, no straight lines.
Have thirty seconds to touch an object of a certain color in the space, no running however.
Change direction only when they come to a wall or another person.

Chapter Eleven
Stage Movement

> *"My playground was the theatre.*
> *I'd sit and watch my mother pretend for a living ... "*
> *— Gwyneth Paltrow*

To be comfortable and successful on-stage it is important for young theatre students to be well practiced in stage geography and movement. They need to be adept at using the nine areas of a conventional stage: the three positions of downstage, the three positions of center stage, and the three positions of upstage. To be effective stage actors they need to know the basic acting positions: full front, full back, one-quarter left and right, three-quarters left and right, and profile left and right.

The following activity works well as a warm-up to review stage geography and movement and give an entire group several opportunities to move around the stage from one position to another and to use a variety of acting positions.

159. Upstage Downstage

At the beginning of a semester, when students are learning stage directions, this is a perfect warm-up.

Materials: Index cards, a basket

Preparation: The teacher and/or students write fifteen to twenty — or more — combinations of stage directions and acting positions on index cards, folded in half, and put in the basket.

A student is chosen to be the director and picks eight to ten students to stand on-stage or in a designated acting area. The students stand in any position on-stage, and the director pulls stage directions out of the hat and reads them aloud. The students follow the direction. The last person to follow the direction or the person who gets into an incorrect position is "cut from the cast" and sits out.

Some examples of stage directions and combinations of directions and acting positions that could be written on cards are:

Upstage left

Downstage right in quarter position, facing stage left

Downstage center, profile, gesture with upstage hand

Upstage right, three-quarters right

Center stage right in quarter position, kneeling on downstage knee

At the teacher's discretion, the directors can be replaced by new ones, and a different group of students can take the stage so that everyone has an opportunity to participate.

Chapter Twelve
Voice

His speech flowed from his tongue sweeter than honey.
— Homer in the Iliad

Patsy Rodenburg, famous voice coach at Britain's Royal National Theatre, tells her acting students that "proper voice work, or the lack of it, could make or break a performer." Whatever work is undertaken to improve the voice, breathing is the key to one that is well-modulated and resonant.

The following poem from *The Actor Speaks: Voice and the Performer* by Patsy Rodenburg describes the importance of conscious breathing for effective voice production:

As you sit waiting to go into rehearsal or audition — breathe.
As the nerves surge through you — breathe.
As you walk onto the stage — breathe.
As you wait for "action" or to respond — breathe.

On exhalation the diaphragm — a large muscle located below the ribs — pushes the air out of the lungs and into the windpipe. The exhaled air causes the vocal cords to vibrate and create sound. The sound created by the vocal cords is weak, however, and must be amplified by the resonators, which are the bones and sinus cavities in the nose, throat, and mouth. Although the resonators can't be changed, the shape, size, and tension of the resonating chambers in the mouth and throat can be, thus adjusting voice quality. The sound created becomes speech when the articulators — the jaw, palate, lips, teeth, and tongue — create words. "Speak the speech, I pray you, as I pronounced it to you, trippingly on the tongue ... " said Hamlet, but words don't come trippingly off the tongue without conscious effort on the part of an actor. Speaking with resonance and clarity requires study and practice.

The human voice has been called the greatest musical instrument ever designed. An actor relies heavily on this priceless instrument so it is important for him to know how the vocal mechanism works and how to use it effectively so that his voice can be easily heard, flexible, and intelligible. An actor can be taught to be comfortably heard in a small group or in front of a large audience. Projection can be improved by proper diaphragmatic breathing and breath control, good posture, and by relaxing the body and vocal mechanism. My wonderful acting teacher once told my classmates and me not to think of our voice as coming from our mouth, but from our lower lungs. "Speak from your gut," she used to say.

Vocal flexibility can be developed by varying pitch, rate, and force. If an actor understands what is being read and has a goal of clear and accurate interpretation of the material, he will vary pitch depending on the ideas communicated, speed up or slow down depending on the mood of the piece, and use emphasis on words or phrases to express meaning.

Intelligibility will become a quality of an actor's voice when he learns to articulate, enunciate, and correctly pronounce words. If the goal is to effectively communicate a playwright's meaning, an actor will do his best to deliver his speeches clearly and distinctly.

Relaxation exercises for the entire body positively influence the voice, but vocal exercises target specific parts of the vocal mechanism and can be easily practiced and are often enjoyable. They can aid an actor in achieving the rich, full speaking voice necessary for a pleasant tone and adequate projection.

This section includes vocal warm-ups that will provide practice in acquiring a rich, flexible voice, interesting to listen to and easy to understand. And don't forget to breathe!

160. Adverb Versatility

The challenge in this vocal warm-up is to accurately communicate certain adverbs by varying pitch, rate, and emphasis.

Materials: A basket, about twenty-five index cards

Preparation: Write descriptive adverbs on the index cards.

Students sit or stand in a circle. The teacher passes around the basket of adverb cards. Each student chooses a card and then is given a sentence to say, such as "There's someone at the door," "Everything is the same," or "Today is Monday." As each student speaks the sentence, the rest of the group listens carefully and tries to accurately determine the adverb expressed. For example, if a student picks "happily" and the chosen sentence is "Everything is the same," he could say it in a slightly higher pitch, brighten his tone, use a lively rate of speaking, put a smile on his face, and position his body with head and shoulders raised. The quicker the group identifies the adverb, the more successful the student has been in communicating the mood and color of the adverb. The warm-up continues until every student has had a chance to exhibit adverb versatility.

Adverbs

Happily	Sarcastically	Sleepily
Haughtily	Sadly	Cautiously
Sternly	Eagerly	Shyly
Loudly	Joyously	Irritably
Excitedly	Anxiously	Frantically
Nastily	Proudly	Quietly
Suspiciously	Enthusiastically	

161. Barney

This is a silly game that encourages voice articulation and quick thinking.

Materials: A small, lightweight ball

Players stand in a big circle. The teacher tosses a ball to a player and says a letter such as "b." That player must come up with the name of a person, a product, and a location, all starting with that letter. For example, the player could quickly and clearly reply, "Barney sells bread in Bulgaria." He then tosses the ball to another player, says a different letter of the alphabet, and the game goes on until everyone has had a chance to offer the name of a person, a product, and a location.

162. Boom Chicka

This is a great game for utilizing a variety of vocal techniques.

The teacher leads the following chant in various ways: as an opera singer, in jive, as a revival preacher, in a whisper, with a sexy voice, fast, slow, with a British accent, or any other variations.

TEACHER: I say *boom.*
STUDENTS: I say *boom.*
TEACHER: I say boom-chicka.
STUDENTS: I say boom-chicka.
TEACHER: I say boom-chicka-boom.
STUDENTS: I say boom-chicka-boom.

TEACHER: I say boom-chicka-rocka-chicka-rocka-chicka-boom.
STUDENTS: I say boom-chicka-rocka-chicka-rocka-chicka-boom.
TEACHER: Oh yeah.
STUDENTS: Oh yeah.
TEACHER: One more time.
STUDENTS: One more time.

Students can also be given the opportunity to lead the chant.

163. Can You Hear Me Now?

In order to be heard, a student uses deep breathing and this warm-up provides the opportunity to do so.

The purpose of this warm-up is for pairs to carry on a conversation as the distance between them increases, so that they can learn to project.

The group is divided into pairs who spread throughout the room and face each other. They can talk about whatever they want, but the challenge is that all the other pairs will be having conversations at the same time. In order to prevent nonsense talk or awkward silences, the pairs are encouraged to brainstorm some topics they can discuss before the conversation begins.

Every thirty seconds a whistle is blown or another signal is given for the students to take a step back from their partners while continuing their conversation. Whenever they hear the signal they take another step back from their partners. When a pair reaches a point where they can no longer hear each other, they should not go back any farther. They should move forward until they find the farthest point at which they can still talk with each other and understand what the other is saying. Projection is the objective. *No screaming allowed.*

164. The Great Wow

This is a fun exercise to get the voice warmed up, and a great energy and spirit booster that can be used before a performance.

The best arrangement for this warm-up is in a fairly tight circle. Everyone starts by kneeling or crouching on the floor and saying in a whisper, "Wow!" Gradually, they straighten up and steadily increase their volume as they repeat, "Wow!" until everyone is standing and stretching as high as they can and saying, with lots of volume supported by the diaphragm, *"Woooow!"*

165. If You Make a Face Like That

The following short sequence of exercises helps to warm up the vocal mechanism. There may be a bit of giggling, which is not surprising because aspects of this warm-up are a bit goofy.

Everyone stands in a circle.

The Gumby Face
Students scrunch up their face really tightly, making it as small as they can. Then they open their mouth as wide as they can and make a huge yawn. Lastly, they make the face their mother always warned them about, "If you make a face like that it'll stay that way."

Chew
Students work their jaw appropriately to whatever is in their mouth. Some chewing options are:
One, two, and three pieces of bubble gum
Super sticky taffy
Carrots
Teeny tiny pretzels
Beef jerky

Noises

Students use the various parts of their vocal mechanism to produce the following unique sounds:

Motor boat, first high and then low

Hum, see how long players can sustain a hum on one breath

A loud noise with open mouth, keep the sound going as the mouth is closed; open mouth and make the loud noise again

A short staccato sound while saying, "ha, ha, ha"

166. Projection Project

The goal of this warm-up is for students to say their lines distinctly and with adequate volume.

Preparation: A copy of the class-created script given to each student.

Students are divided into pairs, arranged in two rows facing each other about three feet apart, and are given their script. One row says lines A and the other row says lines B. After each interchange, the rows take a giant step backwards so that the distance between them increases. The partners should not end up being so far apart that they cannot effectively project and be heard. Screaming is *not* projecting. If either member of the pair cannot hear or understand a line clearly, he can raise his hand to indicate that his partner should try again.

Sample Script:

ROW A: I live in an ice house.

ROW B: I live in a nice house.

ROW A: I go to summer school.

ROW B: I think the summer's cool.

ROW A: I see your two eyes.

ROW B: I see you are too wise.

ROW A: It is five minutes to eight.

ROW B: You have five minutes to wait.

ROW A: Give me some ice.

ROW B: Give me some mice.

Partners alternate saying the following words, making sure there is a distinction between them:

ROW A: Pin.
ROW B: Pen.
ROW A: Kin.
ROW B: Ken.
ROW A: Tin.
ROW B: Ten.
ROW A: Him.
ROW B: Hem.
ROW A: Sit.
ROW B: Set.
ROW A: Big.
ROW B: Beg.
ROW A: Min.
ROW B: Men.
ROW A: Minnie.
ROW B: Many.

Partners alternate practicing these words making sure not to substitute "n" for "ng":
ROW A: Doing.
ROW B: Coming.
ROW A: Nothing.
ROW B: Walking.
ROW A: Talking.
ROW B: Going.
ROW A: Playing.
ROW B: Saying.

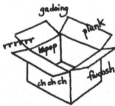

167. Sound Box

What fun the students will have creating unique sounds during this vocal warm-up!

Everyone sits or stands in a circle with heads down and eyes closed. The teacher or a volunteer begins the game by creating a repetitive sound, such as "glug glug glug." The rest of the players randomly chime in, adding their own sounds — clucking, tooting, whistling, humming and so on — until the whole room is filled with sounds. Players are encouraged to make their sounds creative: "ploink ploink ploink," "whoosh whoosh whoosh," "kafloo kafloo kafloo."

When the sound box reaches its peak because all players are sounding off, the first player slows down and stops. The remaining students, *one at a time,* also wind down and stop until the room is silent.

If some students are hesitant to add a sound to the sound box randomly, the sounds could be added one by one, around the circle.

168. Saying Their Own Name

Not only is this a good game for warming up the voice, but it also stimulates quick creation of a character.

The students sit in a big circle on chairs or on the floor. Each is asked to say his name as if:

Correcting someone
Sick with a sore throat
Being tickled
He's lost his voice
Meeting someone famous
He's seen a sad movie
Underwater
Eating a whole peanut butter sandwich without anything to drink
At a concert
Sneezing
In a library
He's just run a race
He's just jumped into a freezing cold pool

169. Shakespearean Insults

Hurling Shakespearean insults is a great way for a young actor to practice vocal technique.

Materials: Index cards and a basket

Preparation: Shakespearean insults — found online — are written on the index cards and put in the basket.

The students are divided into groups of three. Each group picks a card from the basket and goes off to an area of the room to memorize the insult with the intent of being able to "hurl" it at the audience in unison using adequate projection, proper pronunciation, and clear articulation. An incentive for excellence in presentation is to have the audience rate each group on a scale of one to ten for projection, clarity, unity, pronunciation, and vigor.

Insults

Out, you green sickness! Out, you baggage, you tallow face, you worm!

You brawling blasphemous uncharitable dog!

Hang cur, hang you horse, you insolent noise-maker!

Get you gone, you dwarf, you minimus of hindering know-gras made, you bead, you acorn!

Hang off, thou cat, thou burr, vile thing: let loose or I will shake thee from me like a serpent!

Oh me, you juggler, you cancer blossom, you thief of love!

Thou painted Maypole, I am not yet so low that my nails will not reach unto thine eyes!

All the infections that the sun sucks up from bogs, fens, flats on Prospero fall and make him by inchmeal a disease!

170. Sound and Motion

This warm-up simply offers students a humorous way to use their voices.

Players are arranged in pairs facing each other. Without planning ahead, Player A engages in several movements while facing his partner. He could tap his fingers together, suddenly throw open his arms, and then slowly gyrate down to the floor. Player B makes sounds that simultaneously match his partner's movements. For example, Player B might do small rhythmic "tsk-tsk" sounds followed by a sudden yell as Player A throws open his arms, and then a slow exhale sound when his partner moves down to the floor. Next, the players switch roles. Player B makes movements that Player A matches with sounds.

171. Sound Ball

Not only is this a suitable game to use during a unit on voice or to warm up the voice, but it also encourages eye contact, quick creative thinking, and provides a light, physical workout.

Students stand in a circle. The teacher starts the game by throwing an imaginary ball of sound to another person in the circle. A fun sound effect is created to accompany the toss. The student who receives the ball, catches it with the same sound effect, and then tosses it to someone else with a different sound effect. Play continues until everyone has received and thrown the imaginary ball.

172. Soundings

The object of this warm-up is to see how many different sounds can be made with just voices.

Students sit in a circle and do the following:
- Take turns going around the circle saying their names as quickly as they can.
- Say their name as slowly as they can, adding vocal variations.
- Close their eyes. The teacher starts by making a sound like a tongue click, hum, beep, or whistle, and players pass it along from player to player as quickly as possible.
- Each player imitates a sound, such as birds in the forest, waves breaking on the beach, traffic sounds, or musical instruments. The players can either reveal what they are imitating, or create the sound and the group guesses the sound they're making.

To conclude this warm-up, the class is divided into groups of three to five and given several minutes to work together practicing a familiar song using unusual sounds. For example, three frogs singing the tune to *Row Your Boat* by using croaking sounds.

173. Tongue Twister Game

This gives students an opportunity to work hard on making themselves understood, and they love the laughter that's inevitable while playing this game.

Materials: Enough strips of paper for every student, a basket

Preparation: Tongue twisters are written on each strip of paper and put in the basket.

Each student chooses a tongue twister from the basket, goes off somewhere in the room to memorize it, and returns being able to repeat it twice without error. Students then sit or stand in a circle. A volunteer recites his tongue twister twice. The rest of the students listen carefully because the next step is to have the player on the right repeat the tongue twister twice, and so on around the circle. If a player makes a mistake, he sits in the center of the circle. After everyone has repeated the tongue twister twice, every one who was in the center of the circle rejoins the group for the next round and another player offers a new tongue twister that's repeated around the circle. If time permits, a game can be played in which students don't get to rejoin the circle and two students are left standing.

Tongue Twisters
Six slim sleek slender saplings
Selfish shellfish
Red leather, yellow leather
Knapsack straps
Specific Pacific
Burgess's Fish Shop sauce
Men munch much mush
Rush the washing, Russell
Good blood, bad blood
Toy boat
Fresh fried fish
Pre-shrunk shirts
We're your well-wishers

174. Tongue Twisters Together

One of the best ways to exercise the vocal mechanism is by articulating tongue twisters.

Students stand in a circle. The teacher says a tongue twister and the class echoes it. For example:

TEACHER: The bigger the burger,
STUDENTS: The bigger the burger
TEACHER: The better the burger
STUDENTS: The better the burger.
TEACHER: The burgers are better at Burger King.
STUDENTS: The burgers are better at Burger King.
TEACHER: The bigger the burger, the better the burger. The burgers are better at Burger King.
STUDENTS: The bigger the burger, the better the burger. The burgers are better at Burger King.

Other Tongue Twisters

The tip of the tongue the teeth the lips
Unique New York
You know you need unique New York

There are many other delightful tongue twisters that can be used for this warm-up. The students could share one they've learned.

175. Vocal Warm-Up #1

To exercise the vocal mechanism, this warm-up is perfect.

Students stand facing the teacher and are asked to:

• Count aloud to twenty — or any other number — by twos.
• Count from one to fifteen by halves.
• Count by twos to twenty beginning softly and gradually becoming louder, and then vice versa.
• Count to twenty like a drill sergeant, like a small child, like an opera singer, happily, sadly, angrily, shyly, and any other way.

- Make their faces very small, pushing their features into the center of their face with their hands, and then make their faces very big, puffing their cheeks out like an inflated balloon.
- Smile a big, dumb smile. Frown a big, angry frown. Make a huge sneer. Chew a large wad of bubble gum.
- Repeat the sequence, "ah, ay, ee, oh, oo" two or three times. Jaws should be loose and relaxed. The teacher can extend this part of the exercise by having the students add consonants or consonant blends to the beginning or end of the basic vowel sounds. For example, place "t" at the beginning of each sound, producing, "Tah, Tay, Tee, Toh, Too," or place "rt" at the end of each sound producing, "art, ayrt, eert, ohrt, oort."

Bibliography

Books

Caltagirone, Dennis. *Theatre Arts: The Dynamics of Acting.* Lincolnwood, IL: National Textbook Company, 1989.

Casady, Marsh. *Acting Games.* Colorado Springs: Meriwether Publishing Ltd., 1993.

Farmer, David. *101 Drama Games & Activities.* Second Edition. CreateSpace, 2009.

Gregson, Bob. *The Incredible Indoor Games Book.* Evanston, IL: Northwestern Univ. Press, 1986.

Levy, Gavin. *112 Acting Games.* Colorado Springs: Meriwether Publishing Ltd., 2005.

Novelly, Maria C. *Theatre Games for Young Performers.* Colorado Springs: Meriwether Publishing Ltd., 1998.

Peterson, Lenka and Dan O'Conner. *Kids Take the Stage.* New York: Backstage Books, 2006.

Rodenburg, Patsy. *The Actor Speaks.* New York: Pelgrave Macmillan, 2002.

Rubinstein, Robert. *Curtains Up: Theatre Games and Storytelling.* Golden, CO: Fulcrum Resources, 2000.

Schotz, Amiel. *Theatre Games and Beyond.* Colorado Springs: Meriwether Publishing Ltd., 1998.

Spolin, Viola. *Theatre Games for the Classroom.* Evanston, IL: Northwestern University Press, 1986.

Tanner, Fran Averett. *Basic Drama Projects.* Clark Publishing Co., Pocatello, ID, 1973.

Tanner, Fran Averett. *Creative Communication: Junior High Projects in Acting, Speaking, Oral Reading.* Pocatello, ID: Clark Publishing Co., 1973.

Weinstein, Matt and Joel Goodman. *Playfair: Everybody's Guide to Noncompetitive Play.* San Luis Obispo, CA: Impact Publishers, 1980.

Websites

Cambridge Public Schools Drama Collaborative.
http://www.cps.ci.cambridge.ma.us/Web/Curriculum/Drama/index.html.
*Published by the Cambridge Public Schools Drama Collaborative. Presents
useful resources and drama games for the classroom. Click on "Theatre
Games" under "Curriculum Guides."*

Fantastic Plays for Kids. http://www.childdrama.com
*Homepage of Matt Buchanan, playwright and drama teacher. One of the best
sites for theatre games, activities, and lesson plans.*

Creative Drama and Theatre Education Resource Site. http://www.creativedrama.com.
*Detailed source for classroom ideas, production suggestions, and theatre
games.*

Tikhtak's Creative Toolbox.
http://www.creative-toolbox.blogspot.com/search/label game.
Blog space which records warm-up games, icebreakers, and drama exercises.

Gordon's Party Piece. http://www.disbelieving.com.
*Wonderful source for party planners and those in search of group games.
Click on "Planning a Party" and then click "Games to Play."*

FuzzyCo. http://www.fuzzyco.com.
Excellent source for groups and games related to improvisation.

Saldana, Johnny. Games. http://www.geocities.com/shalyndria13/games.
Selected games from various categories.

Improv Encyclopedia. http://www.improvencyclopedia.org.
*One of the best online sites for information on improvisation and improv
games.*

Learnimprov.com. http://www.learnimprov.com.
*Devoted to improvisational comedy theatre. Includes warm-up games and
exercises.*

Primary Resources. http://www.primaryresources.co.uk
*A delightful games site that includes many different kinds of games and
activities originally created for young children, but work with all age groups.*

National Association of Youth Theatres (NAYT).
http://www.nayt.org.uk/support/theatregames.htm.
*National Association of Youth Theatres offers information on youth theatres,
where to find scripts, and an alphabetized list of popular theatre games.*

Party Game Central — Party games and birthday games for kids and adults.
http://www.partygamecentral.com.
A very large party game website.

The Spolin Center. http://www.spolin.com.
Extensive devotion to many subjects related to the work of Viola Spolin.

ABOUT THE AUTHOR:

Nancy Hurley grew up in Orange City, Iowa, home to Northwestern College, where she earned her B.A. in Speech and Theatre. While at Northwestern she was presented with the Alpha Psi Omega dramatics fraternity Best Actress Award and was named to *Who's Who in American Colleges and Universities*. After receiving her M.A. in Speech and Theatre from Eastern New Mexico University, Nancy taught middle school theatre in New Mexico; Ontario, Canada; and southern California.